Read and write
Japanese script

Helen Gilhooly

For UK order enquiries: please contact
Bookpoint Ltd, 130 Milton Park, Abingdon, Oxon, OX14 4SB.
Telephone: +44 (0) 1235 827720. *Fax:* +44 (0) 1235 400454.
Lines are open 09.00–17.00, Monday to Saturday, with a 24-hour message
answering service. Details about our titles and how to order are available at
www.teachyourself.co.uk

For USA order enquiries: please contact
McGraw-Hill Customer Services, PO Box 545,
Blacklick, OH 43004-0545, USA.
Telephone: 1-800-722-4726. *Fax:* 1-614-755-5645.

For Canada order enquiries: please contact
McGraw-Hill Ryerson Ltd, 300 Water St, Whitby,
Ontario, L1N 9B6, Canada.
Telephone: 905 430 5000. *Fax:* 905 430 5020.

Long renowned as the authoritative source for self-guided learning – with
more than 50 million copies sold worldwide – the *Teach Yourself* series
includes over 500 titles in the fields of languages, crafts, hobbies, business,
computing and education.

British Library Cataloguing in Publication Data: a catalogue record for this
title is available from the British Library.

Library of Congress Catalog Card Number: on file.

Previously published in UK 1999 as *Teach Yourself Beginner's Japanese
Script* by Hodder Education, 338 Euston Road, London, NW1 3BH.

Previously published in US 1999 as *Teach Yourself Beginner's Japanese
Script* by The McGraw-Hill Companies, Inc.

This edition published 2010.

The *Teach Yourself* name is a registered trade mark of Hodder Headline.

Typeset by MPS Limited, A Macmillan Company.

Printed in Great Britain for Hodder Education, a division of Hodder
Headline, 338 Euston Road, London, NW1 3BH, by CPI Group (UK) Ltd,
Croydon, CR0 4YY.

The publisher has used its best endeavours to ensure that the URLs for
external websites referred to in this book are correct and active at the time
of going to press. However, the publisher and the author have no respon-
sibility for the websites and can make no guarantee that a site will remain
live or that the content will remain relevant, decent or appropriate.

Hodder Headline's policy is to use papers that are natural, renewable and
recyclable products and made from wood grown in sustainable forests.
The logging and manufacturing processes are expected to conform to the
environmental regulations of the country of origin.

Impression number   10   9   8

Year   2014

Acknowledgements

Thank you to everyone who has advised me on the writing of this book. In particular, to Masae Sugahara and Miyuki Nagai of the School of East Asian Studies, Sheffield University – Masae for the calligraphy and for reading and commenting on the text, Miyuki for the artwork and ideas for mnemonics; to Niamh Kelly of the Japanese Department, Dublin City University, for reading the text and making lots of useful suggestions; Mavis Pilbeam of the Japanese Department of the British Museum for her thorough and very helpful proofreading; Robert Gilhooly for providing the photographs; my students (including Margaret Teasdale) for being 'guinea pigs'; Sue Hart and Carolyn Taylor at Hodder and Stoughton; and John Rogers for doing all the cooking!

The publishers and author would like to thank the following for the use of material in this book: Kyoto Newspaper Company and Nobuko Kogawa (29/10/98) and Kinako Matsumoto, Seikyo Newspaper (14/9/92).

About the author

Helen Gilhooly has lived and worked in Japan, and has extensive experience of teaching Japanese and writing teaching materials at secondary school and adult level. She has an MA and a PGCE in Japanese and is the Language College Director of Aldercar Community Language College in Derbyshire. She is also a teacher trainer of Japanese at Nottingham University. Helen Gilhooly has written *Get started in Japanese*, *Speak Japanese with confidence*, *Complete Japanese*, *World Cultures: Japan* and has co-written and presented *Michel Thomas Method Japanese*, *Foundation* and *Advanced*.

Contents

....

Credits

Front cover: © Oxford Illustrators Ltd.

Back cover and pack: © Jakub Semeniuk/iStockphoto.com,
© Royalty-Free/Corbis, © agencyby/iStockphoto.com, © Andy
Cook/iStockphoto.com, © Christopher Ewing/iStockphoto.com,
© zebicho - Fotolia.com, © Geoffrey Holman/iStockphoto.com,
© Photodisc/Getty Images, © James C. Pruitt/iStockphoto.com,
© Mohamed Saber - Fotolia.com

Pack: © Stockbyte/Getty Images

Only got a minute?

Let's look at the three Japanese scripts:

Kanji 漢字

Kan is an ancient word meaning 'Chinese' and *ji* means 'letter' or 'character', hence *kanji* is translated as 'Chinese characters'. This script was invented by the Chinese and introduced to Japan. *Kanji* are ideographs; this means that the whole character conveys a meaning or idea. For example 月 is the *kanji* for 'moon' and developed like this:

$$\text{图} \rightarrow \text{冃} \rightarrow \text{月} \rightarrow \text{月}$$

Kana かな

The other two scripts are called *hiragana* and *katakana* and are known collectively as *kana*. They are phonetic alphabets or syllabaries, which means that each symbol represents only one sound, unlike the roman alphabet system, where letters are grouped into sounds and the same letter can be pronounced in different ways, as 'a' in 'r<u>a</u>t', 'r<u>a</u>te', 'f<u>a</u>r' and 'f<u>a</u>re'.

This is how it works in Japanese:

The word for 'house' (*uchi*) is made up of two sounds, U-CHI. These sounds are represented by two *hiragana* symbols: うち

Hiragana is used to write the grammatical parts of words and to write non-*kanji* words; *katakana* is used for writing non-Japanese words which have entered the Japanese language. For example, カメラ (*kamera*) means 'camera'.

Read and write Japanese script will enable you to learn Japanese script in easy-to-remember ways and give you the confidence to become a competent reader and writer of Japanese.

5 Only got five minutes?

Learning to read and write Japanese is both an achievable challenge and a hugely satisfying skill to master. The first European visitors to Japan in the 16th century called the Japanese language 'the devil's tongue', but one of the aims of this book is to convince you that this is simply not the case.

So what are the Japanese scripts, and how did they develop? Let's look at this in more detail.

A brief history

The Japanese writing system was introduced into Japan by the Chinese around the middle of the 6th century AD. The Chinese language is very different to Japanese in structure, so the writing system was gradually adapted to fit the structure of the Japanese language. There are now three scripts which make up the Japanese writing system (four if you include rōmaji or roman script, in other words, the Western alphabet).

Kanji 漢字

Kan is an ancient word meaning 'Chinese' and *ji* means 'letter' or character, hence *kanji* is translated as 'Chinese characters'. This was the script which was invented by the Chinese and introduced to Japan. *Kanji* are ideographs; this means that the whole character conveys a meaning or idea (whereas in the roman alphabet system, letters are grouped together to make words). For example 日 is the *kanji* for 'sun'. *Kanji* were originally drawn from pictures of nature and gradually developed into the standardized *kanji* used today. For example 日 sun developed like this:

You will learn more about this in Unit 1.

There is usually more than one pronunciation for a *kanji* character. There are two types of pronunciation, known as *onyomi* (Chinese reading) and *kunyomi* (Japanese reading). You will learn more about this in Unit 2.

Kana かな

The other two scripts in the Japanese writing system are called *hiragana* and *katakana* and are known collectively as *kana*. They are phonetic alphabets or syllabaries, which means that each symbol represents one sound only. This differs from the roman alphabet system, where letters are grouped into sounds and where the same letter can be pronounced in different ways depending on its grouping (e.g. 'a' in 'r<u>a</u>t', 'r<u>a</u>te', 'f<u>a</u>r' and 'f<u>a</u>re'). The difference between the Japanese phonetic system and the alphabet system can be shown through an example:

In English, the word 'house' is made up of five letters: H-O-U-S-E. In Japanese, the word for 'house' (*uchi*) is made up of two sounds, U-CHI. These sounds are represented by two hiragana symbols: うち

The *hiragana* and *katakana* scripts represent the same set of 46 basic sounds, but the symbols are written differently and the two scripts are used for different purposes, as described in the following sections.

Hiragana ひらがな

The word *hiragana* means 'rounded/easy to use' and indicates both the shape and the relative simplicity of the script. Each symbol was developed from simplified *kanji* with the same pronunciation. For example, the *hiragana* symbol か (ka) is a simplified version of the *kanji* 加 (pronounced ka). The left side remains very similar in the *hiragana* symbol, the right-side 'box' has been reduced to a slanting line.

Hiragana is used to write the grammatical parts of words and sentences and to write Japanese words which don't have a *kanji*. For example, when writing verbs (action words), *kanji* is used to express the main idea or meaning and *hiragana* is used to indicate the function of the verb:

'I listen' is written: **聞きます**

The *kanji* 聞 conveys the meaning 'listen'; きます are three *hiragana* which show that the action is present tense.

'I listened' is written: **聞きました**

The same *kanji* 聞 conveys the meaning 'listen'. The four *hiragana* show that it is a past action. You will learn more about this in Units 5 and 10.

Japanese children learn *hiragana* first and then gradually replace words and parts of words with *kanji* as they progress. *Hiragana* is also used to indicate how to pronounce a *kanji* when it is first learned or if it is unusual. When used in this way, it is called *furigana* and is written beside or above the *kanji*.

Katakana カタカナ

The *kata* of *katakana* means 'partial'; this is because each *katakana* symbol was developed from part of a *kanji* with the same pronunciation. For example, the *katakana* symbol カ (ka) comes from the left side of the *kanji* 加 (pronounced ka). (In this example, the same *kanji* is the root of both the *hiragana* and *katakana* symbol; this isn't always the case.)

Katakana script represents the same set of sounds as *hiragana*, but the symbols are written differently and are used for different purposes. In overall appearance, *hiragana* symbols are rounded in shape and *katakana* symbols are more angular. This will become more apparent once you have worked through Units 5 and 9.

Katakana has a number of uses. Firstly, it is used for writing non-Japanese words which have been introduced into the language. These fall into two categories:

1 Loan words For example, ウォークマン (wōkuman) means 'walkman'; テレビ (terebi) means 'television'.

2 Foreign names For example, countries, cities and personal names: アメリカ (amerika) = America; パリ (pari) = Paris; スシス (sumisu) = Smith.

There are also two categories in which *katakana* is used for writing Japanese words:

1 To make words stand out. *Katakana* makes words stand out in a similar way to writing a word in bold, italics or capitals. It is used increasingly in advertising (to make the product stand out), for slang words and exclamations, for pop group names and in headlines. Examples include トヨタ (Toyota) and パチンコ (Pachinko – the Japanese pinball game).

2 The classification of plants and animals.

In Read and write Japanese script, you will be learning to read and write both of the kana scripts; you will also be learning to identify more than 170 single kanji and 230 compound words (words made up of two or more kanji), including signs, names, food and drink, warnings and dates. In addition, you will learn all the rules to write the scripts – the book offers lots of writing practice opportunities. Finally, you will apply your learning to deciphering a variety of texts, such as recipes, weather forecasts, manga cartoons, letters, songs and haiku poetry. This book aims to give you the firm foundations of reading and writing so that you can go on and develop these skills further with confidence.

Reading: a national pastime

Japanese people are avid readers, and you will see people of all ages reading even when standing up on a crowded train. Especially popular are manga cartoon books, and visitors to Japan are often surprised to see adults engrossed in comic books which are regarded as children's reading material in Western countries. However, manga comics are written with themes for all age groups, including stories on politics, economics and law.

Magazines also enjoy huge popularity in Japan across all the age groups and in some ways are the equivalent of tabloid-style newspapers. Weekly photo magazines in particular, such as *Focus* and *Friday*, are full of **sukandaru** (scandal) about famous personalities and political figures.

Japan has the highest readership of newspapers in the world. This is partly due to the very high literacy rate in Japan (close to 100%). More than 90% of newspapers published every day are delivered to home subscribers, and Japan is one of the few countries where there are both morning and evening editions.

Where to start reading

Japanese is traditionally written downwards (**tategaki**), and you begin reading from the top right of a page. This means that books are opened from what we would consider to be the back. However, nowadays, books, newspapers and magazines are often written

Western-style, in horizontal lines (**yokogaki**) from left to right, and in these cases, the book is opened from our idea of the front.

In *Read and write Japanese script*, you will learn to read and write both of the **kana** scripts and to identify more than 170 single **kanji** and 230 compound words (words made up of two or more **kanji**), including signs, names, food and drink, warnings and dates. In addition, you will learn all the rules to write the scripts; the book offers lots of opportunities for writing practice. Finally, you will apply your learning to deciphering a variety of texts, such as recipes, weather forecasts, manga cartoons, letters, songs and haiku poetry. This book aims to give you the firm foundations of reading and writing so that you can go on and develop these skills further with confidence.

About this book

The ten units which make up this book will gradually increase your knowledge of written Japanese. **Units 1–4** introduce mainly kanji which developed from pictures of nature. About 3% of kanji fall into this category, but, as you will learn, they are also used as components of more complex kanji. **Units 4** and **6–8** will teach you how to decipher these more complex kanji, giving you the tools to take your study further on completion of this book. There are plenty of hints to aid your learning, and you will learn to build stories to remember the meanings of the kanji.

Units 8 and **10** give you the chance to put your learning into practice. **Unit 8** introduces you to a number of practical kanji words, such as signs, notices and warnings of the kind you would see all around you in Japan. **Unit 10** introduces a number of reading passages and helps you to decipher them and extract their meaning. You will also encounter different styles of printed and handwritten text.

Two of the units are devoted to teaching the two phonetic scripts: **hiragana (Unit 5)** and **katakana (Unit 9)**. There are lots of practice activities and ideas to help you learn and remember these two scripts. You can leave these units out and come back to them later if you wish to concentrate only on **kanji**, but if you take your study of Japanese further, then a knowledge of these scripts is essential.

There are sections throughout the book which concentrate on how to write Japanese. Again, you may wish to leave these out and concentrate on reading only.

At the end of every unit, you will find either a test or a list of important things to remember. This is so you can evaluate how well you have remembered the 漢字 (**kanji**) you have learned up to that point. Make sure you test yourself before moving on to the next unit and keep an eye on your score in each test – if you score over 80%, then you are definitely ready to move on to the next unit; if you score beween 50% and 80%, you may find it helps to read over the explanations for that unit again; if you find you are scoring below 50%, then read through the explanations in that unit again and try some of the practice activities once more before you move on to the next unit.

Insight boxes

These offer tips to help you learn, highlight the essentials that you need to know in order to progress and help you get to grips with the more difficult aspects of Japanese script. They also offer interesting cultural insights. They will often repeat and add to advice already given – take heed of it, but most of all remember that learning Japanese script is fun!

Pacing yourself

- Remember that it is YOU who sets the pace – keep enjoyment of learning at the top of your agenda!

- Find a balance between moving through the book and revising what you have learned. Don't expect to remember everything (even Japanese people forget **kanji**!) and use the indexes at the back where possible to find words you have forgotten.

- Build up a set of small flashcards with **kanji** on one side and English on the other to test yourself from time to time. Start your own dictionary too by using a notebook or address book to write down new words.

Meet the author

The main aim of *Read and write Japanese script* is to show you that written Japanese can be interesting, challenging and fun to learn. When I first went out to Japan to work in the 1980s, I had never learned to read Japanese and realized very quickly that I needed to be able to decipher the seemingly endless range of signs and scripts around me in order to be able to carry out run-of-the-mill tasks such as finding the exit, working out opening times and ordering from a menu! As my understanding of reading Japanese grew, so did my fascination with Japanese scripts. I began to develop stories and codes to help me decipher and remember the scripts and, once I began teaching Japanese, my students too found these stories and methods invaluable in helping them to learn to read and write Japanese. It is these ideas that I want to share with you in this book in order to make reading and writing Japanese accessible to you. Through a step-by-step approach, you will be able to gradually build up your knowledge of and confidence in reading and writing Japanese scripts.

You will find *Read and write Japanese script* useful if you are planning a trip to Japan, are learning Japanese but haven't taken the plunge into reading and writing, or are simply curious about how a non-alphabet writing system works and want the challenge and satisfaction of being able to 'crack the code' and read Japanese. (It is also a great skill to be able to impress friends and colleagues with!) I think that, as you work through this book, you will become enthused about Japanese scripts and discover that reading Japanese is fascinating, logical and very attainable.

Gambatte kudasai! がんばってください！

Good luck!
Helen Gilhooly

1

第一課
Unit 1

In this unit, you will:
- *learn how Japanese script developed from pictures*
- *learn to read the days of the week*
- *begin to write*

1.1 はじめに Introduction

At the beginning of this book, you learned about the history and development of the Japanese writing system and about the three different scripts or writing forms: ひらがな (*hiragana*), カタカナ (*katakana*), and 漢字 (*kanji*). The focus of Units 1–4 is going to be on 漢字 (*kanji*), and by the end of these four units, you will have learned to recognize 58 漢字 (*kanji*) characters and also to understand the meanings of words made up from combinations of these.

漢字 (*kanji*) characters are ideographs. This means that each character represents a whole object or idea. For example:

日 is the 漢字 (*kanji*) symbol for **sun**
月 is the 漢字 (*kanji*) symbol for **moon**

漢字 (*kanji*) were written originally as pictures of the world which the ancient Chinese saw around them. These pictures were gradually, over time, standardized into regular shapes with rules about how to write them correctly. However, the pictures which each 漢字 (*kanji*) developed from can be very useful in helping you to remember the meanings. Look at these developments:

日 (*sun*) developed something like this:

Insight

As well as sun, it also has the meaning day. These two concepts are connected because the rising and setting of the sun defines a day.

月 (*moon*) developed something like this:

Insight

As well as moon, it can also mean month. These two concepts are connected because the length of a month (28 days) is measured by the progress of each new moon.

You can see from these two examples that 漢字 (*kanji*) do not necessarily have only one meaning but can represent a number of associated ideas.

1.2 Work it out!

The aim of this section is to give you the opportunity to work out for yourself the meanings of 漢字 (*kanji*) by linking them to pictures of the objects they represent. The 漢字 (*kanji*) you will start with all have meanings linked to nature and the world which surrounded the ancient Chinese. To carry out this activity, look at pictures 1–12 that follow, then see if you can link them to the 漢字 (*kanji*) a–l at the foot of this page. Try to match the shape of the pictures to the 漢字 (*kanji*) characters. がんばって (*ganbatte*) – good luck!

1
gold

2
tree

3
wood

4
forest

5
mountain

6
stone

7
fire

8
water

9
bamboo

10
ground

11
river

12
rice field

漢字 (*kanji*)

a 山 **b** 川 **c** 金 **d** 田 **e** 竹 **f** 火
g 木 **h** 林 **i** 森 **j** 水 **k** 土 **l** 石

Check your answers at the back of the book, then look again at the pictures and see if you can envisage how the pictures became the standardized 漢字 (*kanji*) which are used today.

1.3 Linking kanji to pictures 1

There follows an artist's impression of the progression of changes from standardized 漢字 (*kanji*) character back to original picture.

漢字 (*kanji*) **Character**	絵 (*e*) **Picture**	英語 (*eigo*) **English**
山	山 → 山 → 山 → 山	mountain
川	川 → 川 → 川	river
金	金 → 金 → 金 → 金	gold/money
田	田 → 田 → 田	rice field
竹	竹 → 竹 → 竹 → 竹	bamboo
火	火 → 火 → 火	fire
木	木 → 木 → 木	tree
林	林 → 林 → 林	wood
森	森 → 森 → 森	forest
水	水 → 水 → 水 → 水	water

土	土 → 土 → 工	ground
石	石 → 石 → 石	stone
月	月 → 月 → 月 → 月	moon
日	日 → 日 → 日 → ☼	sun

Insight

Did you notice how two trees are used to represent a wood, and three trees a forest? You will learn more about this type of 漢字 (kanji) in Unit 2.

練習一 *Activity 1*

How well can you remember the 漢字 (kanji) and meanings you have learned so far? Test yourself by linking each 漢字 (kanji) with its English meaning. The first one is done for you.

1	山	**a**	water ( )
2	石	**b**	moon ( )
3	火	**c**	earth ( )
4	竹	**d**	river ( )
5	金	**e**	tree ( )
6	水	**f**	forest ( )
7	田	**g**	fire ( )
8	林	**h**	stone ( )
9	川	**i**	sun ( )
10	土	**j**	mountain (1)
11	木	**k**	rice field ( )
12	森	**l**	bamboo ( )

13	日		m	wood
14	月		n	gold

1.4 Days of the week

Look at the 漢字 (*kanji*) that follow and remind yourself of their meanings:

日、月、 火、水、木、金、土

sun, moon, fire, water, tree, gold, earth

These 漢字 (*kanji*) are also used to represent the first part of the words for the days of the week. 日 is the first part of **Sunday**, 月 is the first part of **Monday** and so forth.

Insight

Here are some tips to help you remember which 漢字 (*kanji*) represents which day of the week. The first two are easy!

日	sun represents SUNday
月	moon represents MOONday, or Monday as it has become in English
火	fire represents Tuesday. In English, Tuesday derives from the word Tiw, who was the Norse god of war. If you connect the ideas of war and fire in your mind, then you will remember that FIREday is Tuesday!
水	water represents Wednesday – easy to remember because both start with w!
木	tree represents Thursday – both start with t (but do not confuse with Tuesday)
金	gold/money represents Friday – Friday is often pay day!
土	earth/soil represents Saturday. This is the beginning of the weekend and a good day for working in the garden!

練習二 *Activity 2*

Link the 漢字 (*kanji*) in the left column with the corresponding day of the week in the right.

1	火	**a**	Monday
2	日	**b**	Tuesday
3	土	**c**	Wednesday
4	水	**d**	Thursday
5	月	**e**	Friday
6	金	**f**	Saturday
7	木	**g**	Sunday

1.5 読む練習一 Reading practice 1

Throughout the book, this section will give you opportunities to put into practice and further develop your reading of 漢字 you have learned.

The 漢字 (*kanji*) in Activity 2 represent the first part of the words for the days of the week. In fact, the days of the week are written using three 漢字 (*kanji*) characters. The other two are 曜日 and they represent **day**. You already know 日 and have learned that it can mean **day**. 曜 represents the concept of **weekday**, but simply remember them as together representing the day part of **Monday, Tuesday**, etc.

This is what the complete words for the days of the week look like in 漢字 (*kanji*):

日曜日	Sunday
月曜日	Monday
火曜日	Tuesday
水曜日	Wednesday

木曜日	Thursday
金曜日	Friday
土曜日	Saturday

When two or more 漢字 (*kanji*) are combined in this way to produce new words and meanings, they are called 熟語 (*jukugo*) or **compound words**. You will learn more about these in Unit 2.

Insight

You will often see the days of the week written with the first 漢字 (*kanji*) only, for example, on calendars and diary sheets. This is like writing Mon, Tues, Wed, etc. in English.

練習三 *Activity 3*

The following is part of a music events column from a teenage magazine. Notice that the groups and events are written partly in English script. It is highly fashionable in the Japanese music world (among others) for group names and song titles to be written in English. The effect of the script is often far more important than the meaning of the words. (*Rancid Japan Tour* and *Michelle Gun Elephant* from the extract are just two examples of this!)

The day of the week on which each of the events will take place is written in brackets next to the date (13th–23rd). Now have a go at answering the questions that follow the text.

Insight

Notice that only the first 漢字 (*kanji*) for each of the days of the week is written.

13(水)	③ROTTEN ORANGE TOUR ●場所/渋谷クラブアトロ●料金/前売り￥3,000・当日￥3,500(1ドリンク、1CD付)●時間/OPEN17：00・START18：00●出演/GARLIC BOYS、YELLOW MACHINGUN、ダッフルズ他。☎SMASH WEST☎06-361-0313
15(金)	RANCID JAPAN TOUR 1999 ●場所/赤坂BLITZ●料金/￥5,800●時間/OPEN17：00・START18：00●アルバム「LIFE WON'T WAIT」を引っ提げてのツアー。16、23、24日もBLITZでライブをやるぞ。☎クリエイティブマン☎03-5466-0777
15(金)	ゴスペラーズ 1999ゴスペラーズ坂ツアー "アカペラ人" ●場所/シアターアプル●料金/￥5,500(全席指定)●時間/OPEN17：30・START17：30●この日以外も16、17、19、21日の計5日間、同会場でライブが行われる。☎ディスクガレージ☎03-5436-9600
17(日)	THE MICHELLE GUN ELEPHANT「WORLD PCHYCO BLUES TOUR "ALL STANDING／MAXIMUM.!!"」 ●場所/横浜アリーナ●料金/￥4,200●時間/OPEN16：00・START18：00●アルバム「ギヤ・ブルース」が大好評のミッシェルの怒涛のスタンディングツアー。☎ディスクガレージ☎03-5436-9600
19(火)	DOWN BEAT ●場所/西麻布YELLOW●料金/￥2,500(フライヤー持参で￥2,000・共に2ドリンク付)●時間/OPEN・START21：00●出演/DJ KEN-BO、KOYA、ATSUSHI出演のHIP HOPイベント。☎YELLOW☎03-3479-0690
21(木)	Lauryn Hill JAPAN TOUR ●場所/日本武道館●料金/S：￥7,000・A：￥6,000●時間/START19：00●ソロアルバムが世界中で大ヒット中の彼女の待望のソロライブ。22、23日にもライブあり。☎ウドー音楽事務所☎03-3402-5999
21(木)	ZEPPET STORE「COMING UP ROSES TOUR'98」 ●場所/渋谷CLUB QUATTRO●料金/￥3,800●時間/OPEN18：00・START19：00●橋本công文プロデュースのシングル「ROSE」が好評のZEPPET STOREのツアー。☎バックステージTOKYO☎03-3357-8080
22(金)	Breath『3ヶ月無料ライブ』 ●場所/恵比寿ギルティ●料金/無料●時間/OPEN18：30・START19：00●ハードなライブが魅力のバンド、Breathが現在3ヶ月無料ライブを実施中。入場方法などは、インフォメーション☎03-5467-2544まで問い合わせてみてね。
23(土)	WORLD CONNECTION "KOOL" ●場所/西麻布YELLOW●料金/￥3,000(フライヤー持参で￥2,500・共に2ドリンク付)●時間/OPEN・START21：00●出演/DJ：KO KIMURA、FUJIMOTO VJ：E-MAIL●YELLOW☎03-3479-0690

On which day of the week do the following events take place?

1 Rotten Orange Tour

2 Down Beat

3 The Michelle Gun Elephant . . . Tour

4 Rancid Japan Tour

5 World Connection 'Kool'

How many events are taking place on . . .

6 a Friday?

7 a Saturday?

8 a Thursday?

9 Which day of the week is not represented in the events extract?

1.6 書く練習一 Writing practice 1

This section will introduce you to some simple rules for writing 漢字 (*kanji*). You will learn some further rules in Unit 2 and will then practise writing some of the 漢字 (*kanji*) you have learned.

The rules for writing 漢字 (*kanji*) are very precise, and Japanese children spend many hours of their school life learning and practising the correct order for writing each 漢字 (*kanji*). (In a similar way, we learn how to write the letters of the alphabet correctly at school.) Each single part of a 漢字 (*kanji*) is called a stroke, and the order in which 漢字 (*kanji*) are written is called 書 き 順 (*kakijun*) or *stroke order*.

The Japanese use squared paper when they are learning how to write because it helps to ensure that 漢字 (*kanji*) are all the same size and are balanced correctly. If you can, use large-squared graph paper which is subdivided into four smaller squares during the initial stages of learning to write. This will help you to balance left and right, top and bottom of each 漢字 (*kanji*). Alternatively, you could use ordinary graph paper and have four smaller squares making up one larger square. You will also see the 漢字 (*kanji*) taught in the earlier units written in this type of square so that you can copy exactly from the book. Once you feel confident, you can use clear squares or use smaller-squared paper/graph paper for practising and perfecting your technique.

Here are some simple rules to get you started and examples to copy.

Rule 1: Horizontal 漢字 (*kanji*) strokes are written from left to right.

例 (*rei*) Example: **three**

Rule 2: Vertical 漢字 (*kanji*) strokes are written from top to bottom.

例 (*rei*) Example: **river**

Rule 3: Where the 漢字 (*kanji*) character has an intersecting horizontal and vertical stroke, the starting stroke is usually the horizontal one (but there are some exceptions).

例 (*rei*) Example: **earth**

Notice you work downwards; the final stroke is the bottom horizontal one.

Rule 4: A left-hand diagonal line is written before a right-hand diagonal line.

例 (*rei*) Example: **tree**

Rule 5: Here is a square 漢字 (*kanji*).

Rule 6: When the square contains other strokes within it, you fill in this part before writing the bottom line of the square.

例 (rei) Example: **sun**

You can combine these rules you have learned to write 石 (**stone**):

Using these six rules, you have learned to write the following 漢字 (*kanji*) in this section:

三、 川、 土、 木、 日、 石
(**three, river, earth, tree, sun, stone**)

Now see if you can write them on squared paper in the correct order from memory (refer back to the rules to check when you have finished).

Insight

Although it is important to understand and apply the basic rules for writing 漢字 (*kanji*), there are some aspects of stroke order which do not fall easily into rules, so you also need to learn and practise the stroke order for each 漢字 (*kanji*) character. Do not be daunted by this, however –

'practice makes perfect' and if you write 漢字 (*kanji*) over and over again and concentrate on the correct stroke order, you will begin to develop a feel for the order in which they are written.

Insight

You will also begin to develop your own way of remembering and to apply this to writing more complicated 漢字 (*kanji*). In the meantime, you will be given lots of help and advice in the writing sections of this book. In addition, the unit summaries at the back of the book give the stroke order for the main 漢字 (*kanji*) taught in each unit.

1.7 終りに Conclusion

This section in each unit will summarize the main aspects of the unit. In this unit, you have learned 14 漢字 (*kanji*), seven compound words (days of the week) and six basic rules for writing 漢字 (*kanji*).

The following terms and sub-headings have been used in this unit:

第一課	dai ikka	unit 1
はじめに	hajime ni	introduction
漢字	kanji	kanji (Chinese characters)
練習	renshū	activity/practice
読む練習	yomu renshū	reading practice
書く練習	kaku renshū	writing practice
例	rei	example
終りに	owari ni	conclusion

Other key words and terms are given in the conclusion of Unit 2. Refer to these if you want to say the terms and sub-headings used throughout this book in Japanese.

1.8 Five things to remember

At the end of every unit, you will either find a test so that you can evaluate how well you have remembered the 漢字 (*kanji*) you have learned up to that point or a list of important things to remember. Make sure you test yourself before moving on to the next unit and keep an eye on your score (see the **About this book** section for score diagnosis).

Five important things to remember from Unit 1:

- The *kanji* for **sun** 日 also means **day**.
- The *kanji* for **moon** 月 also means **month**.
- Look for the pictures from which *kanji* developed.
- Visually, *kanji* have one <u>main</u> meaning, but there is more than one way of pronouncing them.
- You can pick out some meaning from texts even if you can't read all the script.

2

第二課
Unit 2

In this unit, you will:

- *add some new 漢字 (kanji) to the 14 you have learned already*
- *learn the Japanese pronunciation of these 漢字 (kanji)*
- *apply your learning to real reading situations*
- *learn more about writing Japanese script*

2.1 はじめに Introduction

1 Can you remember the meanings of the 漢字 you were introduced to in Unit 1? You can see them in the following list, so test yourself and check back to Unit 1 if there are any you are unsure about.

山 川 日 月 土 竹 森 木 水 田 金 林
火 石

2 Can you remember which 漢字 represents which day of the week? They are listed below in their full form. Remember, it is the first 漢字 which tells you which day of the week it is.

月曜日 日曜日 土曜日 木曜日 火曜日
水曜日 金曜日

Again, check back to Unit 1 if you are unsure of any them.

2.2 Work it out!

In this section, as with Unit 1, you will be introduced to some new 漢字 through the pictures of natural objects that they are derived from. Most of the 漢字 introduced in this unit are associated with the human body. Try matching the pictures below (1–12) with the 漢字 (a–l) (without looking at the answers!).

> **Insight**
> In two cases (eye and car/vehicle), you may need to imagine the pictures turned on their side to identify them.

| 1 | 2 | 3 | 4 |
| gate | horse | ear | child |

| 5 | 6 | 7 | 8 |
| woman | mouth | eye | foot |

| 9 | 10 | 11 | 12 |
| hand | power | car/vehicle | person |

a 口	b 足	c 目	d 女	e 子	f 人
g 耳	h 手	i 力	j 車	k 馬	l 門

2.3 Linking kanji to pictures 2

There follows an artist's impression of the changes from standardized 漢字 back to picture. Check your answers to the previous activity with this sequence.

漢字	絵(e) Picture	英語 (eigo) English
人 人 → → →		person
女 女 → → →		woman
子 子 → → →		child
目 目 → → →		eye
耳 耳 → → →		ear
口 口 → → →		mouth
手 手 → → →		hand
足 足 → →		foot
力 力 → → →		power/strength
馬 馬 → → →		horse
車 車 → → →		cart/vehicle/car
門 門 → → →		gate

Insight

In this set of new 漢字, there is an example of an abstract noun – 力 (power/strength) – being portrayed in picture form through the image of the muscles in the arm.

車 (vehicle) originally developed from the picture of a cart which would have been the type of transport or vehicle used when 漢字 were first developed. In modern times, it has taken on the meaning of car.

2.4 Kanji build-up

This section in this unit (here and throughout the book) will introduce you to new 漢字 and new words based on the 漢字 you have learned so far.

1 Complex kanji

The pictorial 漢字 that you have been introduced to so far not only have meanings in themselves but are also used as parts or components of 漢字 that are more complex. You actually learned two of these more complex 漢字 in Unit 1. They were 林 (*wood*) and 森 (*forest*). Both are created from 木 (*tree*) – two trees represent a wood, three trees a forest. Here are four more 漢字 built from simpler ones which you have learned already. The meanings of the components are incorporated into these complex 漢字 forms.

Insight

Notice that the simpler 漢字, when used as components of more complex 漢字, may change their shape slightly or appear 'squashed'.

男 (*man*) This is made from the components 田 (*rice field*) and 力 (*power*). In other words, the man uses his power to work in the rice fields.

好 (like, love)　　This is a combination of 女 (woman) and 子 (child). The abstract idea of love is expressed through the love between a woman and her child.

明 (bright)　　This is a combination of 日 (sun) and 月 (moon). The sun and moon shining together would create a very bright light.

本 (root, origin)　　木 (tree) with a horizontal line through the trunk indicates the root of the tree.

Unit 4 will look at these complex 漢字 in more detail, but you can see from these examples that a knowledge of the simpler 漢字 can also help you to decipher the more complex ones.

2 Kanji compounds

The four 漢字 you have just been introduced to are created by combining simpler 漢字 to form one complex 漢字. Another way in which 漢字 are used to create new meanings is by forming words from two or more separate 漢字. You have already been introduced to this idea through the days of the week. Three separate 漢字 are used to make up each day. For example, 月曜日 means **Monday**. Here are some more examples:

人口　　means **population** ('people's mouths' = number of mouths to feed)

馬力　　means **horse power**

女子　　means **girl** ('woman child')

Insight

Notice that 女子 are two separate 漢字, unlike 好 (complex 漢字) which means love/like.

日本　　means **Japan** ('Sun's root' describes Japan as the place east of China where the sun rises. This is where the term 'land of the rising sun' comes from.)

To summarize, 漢字 can join together and form one 漢字, e.g. 男 (referred to as complex 漢字) or they can form words made up of two or more 漢字, e.g. 人口 (referred to as compound 漢字).

練習一 *Activity 1*

Some compound words made up of two or three 漢字 follow. Can you work out their meanings? (You may want to look back at the 漢字 you have learned so far in Units 1 and 2 and refresh your memory before trying this activity.)

a 水力　　**b** 男子　**c** 日本人　**d** 馬車　**e** 人力
f 人力車　**g** 水田　**h** 火山　　**i** 門口　**j** 人目

Once you have thought about possible meanings of these words, look at the list of English words that follows and decide which best fits each 漢字 above before you check the answers at the back of the book.

1 volcano　　　**2** boy　　　　　　　**3** Japanese person
4 carriage　　 **5** in the public eye　**6** water power
7 gateway　　　**8** manpower
9 a rickshaw (man-pulled carriage)
10 a paddy field (a field flooded with water for wet rice growing)

2.5 Working out the meaning

You will have noticed that sometimes the meanings are a direct 'translation' of the separate 漢字 into their new meaning. For example, 火山 ('fire mountain' or *volcano*). In other cases, you need to think more laterally or abstractly. For example, 人目 (*in the public eye*). However, once you know what the meanings are, they are easy to remember, because the pictorial 漢字 act as a visual jog to the memory. And words are created in a very logical fashion. For example, 人力車 means literally human-powered vehicle and that is what a rickshaw is, as the following illustration shows.

Insight

In fact, the English word rickshaw is a corruption of the Japanese word jin-riki-sha. Jin (person) has been dropped, and the other two words (power, vehicle) have had their pronunciation 'anglicized'. Try saying the Japanese rikisha and you'll see what I mean!

2.6 復習 Review

Before continuing any further, here is an activity to help you review the single 漢字 learned so far in this unit.

Match the following 漢字 with their English meanings from the selection in the box. Then try the activity in reverse by taking the English meanings from the box first.

人、力、車、耳、女、明、口、子、男、
好、手、目、馬、門、本、足

If there are any of these characters that you are not sure about, look back through the unit and check your answers.

2.7 読む練習二 Reading practice 2

The way in which dates are written in Japanese is interesting. You were introduced to the 漢字 for moon 月 and sun 日 in Unit 1 and you also learned that these 漢字 have the connected meanings of day 日 and month 月 – so let us look at how this works in practice. This is how a typical Japanese calendar looks for the month of January:

1月[a]

日	月	火	水	木	金	土[b]
1 日	2 日	3 日	4 日	5 日	6 日	7 日[c]
8 日	9 日	10 日	11 日	12 日	13 日	14 日
15 日	16 日	17 日	18 日	19 日	20 日	21 日
22 日	23 日	24 日	25 日	26 日	27 日	28 日
29 日	30 日	31 日				

a is the month written in numerals and 漢字. Japanese months do not have a name as such, so they are assigned a number from 1 to 12. Therefore, 6月 is **June** (the sixth month), 1月 is **January** (the first month) and 12月 is **December**.

b are the 漢字 for the days of the week (as you learned in Unit 1). They are shortened in this case to just the first 漢字 of the three which you learned (for example, 水曜日 means **Wednesday**) because this is all that is needed to identify each day of the week. (This is rather like writing **Tues**, **Wed**, etc. in English.)

c are the days of the month. Each number is followed by 日 (similarly in English we follow the dates with **st**, **nd**, **rd** or **th**, e.g. **1st**, **7th**).

練習二 *Activity 2*

Using the calendar and information just given, try answering the following questions.

1 On which day of the week is the **a** 1st **b** 4th **c** 9th **d** 14th?
2 How many dates in the month fall on a Wednesday, and what are they?
3 On which day of the week will 1月1日 fall?

Insight

Japanese dates are always written in this order: month then date then day of week.

練習三 *Activity 3*

On the next page is a calendar from a Japanese travel brochure. Look at it and answer these questions.

1 What are the starting and finishing months on this calendar?
2 In which months do the following happen?

   a the 2nd is a Tuesday
   b the 24th is a Monday
   c the 6th is a Friday

3 On what day of the week is are the following dates?

a May 5th
b October 26th
c February 18th
d August 21st
e December 25th

4 On what days of the week do these Japanese festivals fall?

    a Girls' Day (March 3rd)
    b New Year's Day
    c Tanabata (Star Festival, July 7th)
    d Golden Week (April 29th–May 5th)
    e Emperor's Birthday (December 23rd)?

4月

日	月	火	水	木	金	土
	1	2	3	4	5	6
7	8	9	10	11	12	13
14	15	16	17	18	19	20
21	22	23	24	25	26	27
28	29	30				

5月

日	月	火	水	木	金	土
			1	2	3	4
5	6	7	8	9	10	11
12	13	14	15	16	17	18
19	20	21	22	23	24	25
26	27	28	29	30	31	

6月

日	月	火	水	木	金	土
						1
2	3	4	5	6	7	8
9	10	11	12	13	14	15
16	17	18	19	20	21	22
23/30	24	25	26	27	28	29

7月

日	月	火	水	木	金	土
	1	2	3	4	5	6
7	8	9	10	11	12	13
14	15	16	17	18	19	20
21	22	23	24	25	26	27
28	29	30	31			

8月

日	月	火	水	木	金	土
				1	2	3
4	5	6	7	8	9	10
11	12	13	14	15	16	17
18	19	20	21	22	23	24
25	26	27	28	29	30	31

9月

日	月	火	水	木	金	土
1	2	3	4	5	6	7
8	9	10	11	12	13	14
15	16	17	18	19	20	21
22	23	24	25	26	27	28
29	30					

10月

日	月	火	水	木	金	土
		1	2	3	4	5
6	7	8	9	10	11	12
13	14	15	16	17	18	19
20	21	22	23	24	25	26
27	28	29	30	31		

11月

日	月	火	水	木	金	土
					1	2
3	4	5	6	7	8	9
10	11	12	13	14	15	16
17	18	19	20	21	22	23
24	25	26	27	28	29	30

12月

日	月	火	水	木	金	土
1	2	3	4	5	6	7
8	9	10	11	12	13	14
15	16	17	18	19	20	21
22	23	24	25	26	27	28
29	30	31				

1月

日	月	火	水	木	金	土
			1	2	3	4
5	6	7	8	9	10	11
12	13	14	15	16	17	18
19	20	21	22	23	24	25
26	27	28	29	30	31	

2月

日	月	火	水	木	金	土
						1
2	3	4	5	6	7	8
9	10	11	12	13	14	15
16	17	18	19	20	21	22
23	24	25	26	27	28	

3月

日	月	火	水	木	金	土
						1
2	3	4	5	6	7	8
9	10	11	12	13	14	15
16	17	18	19	20	21	22
23/30	24/31	25	26	27	28	29

練習四 *Activity 4*

Convert the following dates into English as in the examples.
Remember the Japanese order: **month, date, day.**

例　*Rei* 1　8月3日（火）　= Tuesday 3rd August
　　　　　　　　　　　　　（order: August 3rd Tuesday）

例　*Rei* 2　10月26日（金）　= Friday 26th October

a 2　月 14 日（土）　　　b 11 月 20 日（木）

c 5　月 5 日（月）　　　　d 9　月 10 日（日）

e 12 月 25 日（水）　　　f 4　月 1　日（金）

2.8 漢字の読み方 How to read kanji

This section will teach you about reading 漢字 aloud in Japanese. As suggested at the beginning of the book, if you wish to focus on just understanding the meaning of 漢字, then you can omit these sections as you go through the book or come back to them later.

1 *Kunyomi* (訓読み) and *onyomi* (音読み)

At the beginning of the book, you learned that there are two ways of reading 漢字 in Japanese: the *kunyomi* (訓読み), or Japanese reading, and the *onyomi* (音読み), or Chinese reading. The onyomi has developed from the original Chinese pronunciation, but over the centuries it has been adapted to and become part of the Japanese language. The kunyomi is the native Japanese word.

For example, 川 (**river**) can be pronounced SEN (*onyomi*) and *kawa* (*kunyomi*). Kawa was the Japanese word for **river,** so when 漢字 were introduced from China, this word was linked to the 漢字 character 川.

Insight

Notice that, when written in rōmaji (romanized script or alphabet), kawa (kunyomi) is written in lower case and SEN (onyomi) in upper case. This system is used in many 漢字 workbooks and dictionaries and is also followed in this book.

2 Rules for using kunyomi and onyomi

As a general rule, the kunyomi is used for single 漢字 words whereas the onyomi is used for compound 漢字 words of two or more 漢字. Here is an illustration of this.

a Single 漢字 words

人 (**person**) is pronounced *hito* (*kunyomi*)

口 (**mouth**) is pronounced *kuchi* (*kunyomi*)

b Compound 漢字 words

The above 漢字 make up the compound word 人口 (population) which is pronounced JINKŌ.

JIN and KŌ are the *onyomi* of 人 and 口 respectively.

Insight

There are exceptions to the rules about when to use kunyomi and onyomi, but these will be pointed out to you and explained when necessary, and there will be lots of reinforcement activities, too.

There will be further examples and the opportunity to practise new information and rules as you progress through the book, so don't worry if you've understood only some of the details so far.

練習五 Activity 5

In this unit, you are going to concentrate on the *kunyomi* (Japanese reading) only. In the following list are the 漢字 you learned in Unit 1 with their *kunyomi* and a guide to how to pronounce these readings. Look over these and practise saying them. Then see how well you can remember them by covering up the *kunyomi* column, looking at the 漢字 and saying them from memory.

漢字	*Meaning*	*Kunyomi*	*Pronunciation*
山	mountain	yama	ya-ma (a of mat)
川	river	kawa	ka-wa (a of mat)
金	gold/money	kane	ka-ne (a of mat, e of end)
田	rice field	ta	ta (a of mat)
竹	bamboo	take	ta-ke (a of mat, e of end)
火	fire	hi	(i of hit)
木	tree	ki	(i of hit)
林	wood	hayashi	ha-ya-shi (a of mat, i of hit)
森	forest	mori	mo-ri (o of hot, i of hit)
水	water	mizu	mi-zu (i of hit, u of blue)
土	ground	tsuchi	tsu-chi (tsu is one syllable, chi of chin)
石	stone	ishi	i-shi (i of hit)
月	moon	tsuki	tsu-ki (tsu is one syllable, i of hit)
日	sun	hi	(i of hit)

Insight

Pronunciation rules

There are five vowel sounds in Japanese. These are *a, i, u, e* and *o*. They are always pronounced in the same way.

A general guide to their pronunciation can be seen in the list just given and can be summarized as follows:

- a as in mat
- i as in hit
- u as in blue

- e as in end
- o as in hot

These vowels are attached to consonants to make new sounds – but remember, the pronunciation of each vowel remains constant. The sound **tsu** is a relatively unfamiliar one in English – it is one beat, or syllable: 'squash' the **t** and **s** together as you say it, as in **tsunami**.

You may have noticed that the pronunciation of 火 (**fire**) and 日 (**day/sun**) are the same – *hi*. There are many examples of Japanese words which have the same pronunciation but are written with different 漢字. The difference in meaning can be understood from looking at the 漢字 or from the context. There are many examples in English, too, of words which are pronounced in the same way but which have different meanings, e.g. **here** and **hear**. These differences in meaning are indicated by the spelling or the context or both.

練習六 *Activity 6*

How well can you remember the *kunyomi* reading and pronunciation of each 漢字? You may want to look back at the previous list and practise saying them out aloud – looking at the 漢字 as you do so – before trying the following activities.

A Tick the correct 漢字:

		a	b	c
1	*ta*	竹	田	川
2	*mori*	土	林	森
3	*ishi*	金	石	土
4	*kawa*	川	山	水
5	*ki*	日	火	木

28

B This time, tick the correct kunyomi:

1 金   **a** *kane*   **b** *kawa*   **c** *ki*

2 竹   **a** *ta*   **b** *hayashi*   **c** *take*

3 月   **a** *tsuchi*   **b** *tsuki*   **c** *ishi*

4 林   **a** *hayashi*   **b** *ki*   **c** *mori*

5 水   **a** *mori*   **b** *kawa*   **c** *mizu*

C Now test your understanding of the three aspects of 漢字 you have learned – the 漢字 itself, the *kunyomi* and the meaning in English. You will link these three aspects by choosing one from each of two categories (a–c and i–iii) to match the first item, as in the examples:

例 **Rei** 1   ta   **a** 月   **b** 日   **c** 田 ✓
               i rice field ✓   **ii** moon   **iii** gold

例 **Rei** 2   月   **a** *tsuki* ✓   **b** *tsuchi*   **c** *hi*
               i day   **ii** moon ✓   **iii** earth

1   fire   **a** 水   **b** 木   **c** 火
         i *ki*   **ii** *hi*   **iii** *mizu*

2   森   **a** *mori*   **b** *hayashi*   **c** *ishi*
         i wood   **ii** tree   **iii** forest

3   yama   **a** 川   **b** 竹   **c** 山
         i mountain   **ii** river   **iii** wood

4   gold   **a** 木   **b** 金   **c** 火
         i *kawa*   **ii** *kane*   **iii** *mori*

5   竹   **a** wood   **b** bamboo   **c** river
         i *take*   **ii** *tsuki*   **iii** *tsuchi*

6   *mizu*   **a** water   **b** moon   **c** forest
         i 火   **ii** 木   **iii** 水

7   stone   **a** 田   **b** 石   **c** 日
         i *ishi*   **ii** *tsuchi*   **iii** *ki*

8 土   **a** sun   **b** moon   **c** earth
            i *tsuchi*   **ii** *tsuki*   **iii** *ishi*

9 *kawa*   **a** 川   **b** 水   **c** 竹
            i bamboo   **ii** gold   **iii** river

10 林   **a** wood   **b** forest   **c** tree
            i *mori*   **ii** *hayashi*   **iii** *ki*

練習七 *Activity 7*

This activity gives you the opportunity to use the *kunyomi* for 漢字 learned so far in a real reading situation. Japanese surnames are made up of either single 漢字 or two or three compounded together. The 漢字 used in surnames are often fairly simple ones, including some of those you have learned in Units 1 and 2.

Insight

• Although 漢字 used in surnames have literal meanings (for example, the surname 竹山 (Takeyama) literally means bamboo mountain), the Japanese do not think of them in this way. Many English surnames also have literal meanings (for example, Rivers, Hill, Archer) but again, they are known as names not meanings.

• When saying Japanese surnames, you use the kunyomi. You learned at the beginning of this section that, in general, the onyomi is used for compound 漢字 words. However, names are an exception to this rule.

1 Can you say these common surnames in Japanese?

a 林   **b** 森田   **c** 森山   **d** 山川

e 竹山   **f** 森   **g** 木田   **h** 石川

2 For the following surnames, 田 is pronounced da instead of ta. How do you say these names?

a 金田   **b** 竹田   **c** 石田   **d** 山田   **e** 川田

2.9 書く練習二 Writing practice 2

In Unit 1, you learned some basic rules for writing 漢字. Now you are going to revise these rules with some new 漢字 you have learned in this unit. You will also learn some further rules and, once you are familiar with these, you will have a go at writing 漢字 in the correct order.

Rules 1–3: You learned in Unit 1 that you write from left to right and from top to bottom. Usually, where two lines intersect, the highest horizontal line is written before the vertical line, and then you work downwards. Look at the way you write **hand**. Note that the short top stroke is written from right to left.

Rule 4: Diagonal lines follow the same rule of writing the left diagonal before the right, e.g. **person**.

Rule 5: You also learned in Unit 1 how to write a square. This is how **mouth** is written (notice that the shape is different from the square).

Rule 6: When there is a middle part to the square, you write the bottom line last, e.g. **eye.**

Look too at **rice field** (but notice this is an exception to Rule 3, because the vertical intersecting line inside the square is written before the horizontal).

Here are two further rules.

Rule 7: Where a 漢字 has a distinct left and right part, the left section is written before the right; where it has a distinct top and bottom part, the top section is written first, e.g. **wood.**

Note that the left section is narrower than the right.

And **forest** is similar.

You combine Rules 5, 6 and 7 to write **gate**.

Rule 8: Where a 漢字 is symmetrical with a central 'axis', you write the 'axis' first followed by the left side and then the right side, e.g. **water**.

And **mountain** is a similar instance:

練習八　*Activity 8*

Can you write the following 漢字 applying the rules you have been introduced to so far? Remember to use squared paper to achieve the right balance and proportions.

Rules 1–4:

川 (*river*)　三 (*three*)　力 (*power*)　人 (*person*)

Rules 5 and 6:

日 (*sun*)　月 (*moon*)　田 (*rice field* – exception to Rule 3)

Rule 7:

林 (*wood*)　竹 (*bamboo*)

Rule 8:

小 (*small* – Unit 6)　水 (*water*)　山 (*mountain*)

You can check your answers by looking back through the writing sections of Units 1 and 2. For 力, 月, 竹 look up their stroke order in the unit-by-unit 漢字 charts at the back of this book.

Then use the writing sections and charts for Units 1 and 2 to practise writing all the 漢字 you have learned so far.

> **Insight**
> The rules given in these two units will give you general guidance in most cases, but they are not exhaustive, so pay attention to the stroke order for individual 漢字 and remember that there are exceptions to rules.

2.10 終りに Conclusion

In this unit, you have been introduced to 16 new single 漢字, as well as 14 compound 漢字 words and 13 Japanese surnames. You have also learned to read dates and have been introduced to the readings of some 漢字. And you have reviewed writing rules and learned two new ones.

The following new terms and sub-headings have been used in this unit:

復習	fukushū	review
漢字の読み方	kanji no yomikata	kanji readings
訓読み	kunyomi	Japanese reading
音読み	onyomi	Chinese reading
テスト	tesuto	test

2.11 テスト Test yourself

This section is designed to test how well you have remembered what you have learned in Units 1 and 2.

1 The 漢字 below are grouped by theme. Which is the odd one out?

a Parts of the body: 目、足、男、手、耳

b Days of the week: 月、土、火、水、日、林

c People and animals: 馬、子、力、男、女

d Abstract ideas: 好、金、明、力

2 What do these compound 漢字 words mean? (f is a new word.)

a 人口   **b** 日本   **c** 女子
d 門口   **e** 火山   **f** 男女

3 Match these dates (a–g) to the festivals and holidays (i–vii).

a 12月25日   **i** April Fool's Day (1st April)

b 1月1日   **ii** Christmas Day (25th December)

c 7月4日   **iii** Halloween (31st October)

d 3月21日   **iv** May Day (1st May)

e 4月1日   **v** Spring Equinox (21st March)

f 10月31日   **vi** New Year's Day (1st January)

g 5月1日   **vii** American Independence Day (4th July)

4 Can you say these Japanese surnames? (* indicates a change in pronunciation from *ta* to *da*)

a 山田*   **b** 竹山   **c** 森田   **d** 森   **e** 石田*

5 Can you write the following 漢字 in the correct stroke order?

土、日、目、手、木、水、山、田

3

第三課
Unit 3

In this unit, you will:
- *learn to read numbers in Japanese*
- *use these numbers in real reading situations*
- *practise writing 漢字*

3.1 はじめに Introduction

In Unit 2, you learned how to read dates. You are now going to review this by reading the following dates. Choose the English equivalent from the selection below the dates. (Remember that the order in Japanese is month, date, day.)

a 4月21日 (火)   **b** 11月5日 （土）   **c** 9月10日 （水）

i Wednesday 21 April
ii Wednesday 10 September

iii Tuesday 21 April
iv Saturday 5 November

Insight
If you are still unsure about reading dates, then look back at the section on dates in Unit 2 (Section 2.7) to refresh your memory.

3.2 Numbers 1–10

Two systems of numbering have already been used in this book. One of these is the arabic number system (1, 2, 3 . . .). This system is internationally recognized and is used widely in Japan. However, every language has its own words when counting (English: *one, two, three* . . . ; French: ***un, deux, trois*** . . . ; etc.). In Japanese, there are 漢字 which represent the words for numbers. They have been used alongside arabic numbers in this book to number activities and explanations. These are the 漢字 numbers 1–10:

一、二、三、四、五、六、七、八、九、十

The following section (**Remembering the numbers 1**) gives some tips for memorizing these 漢字, and you may already have thought of some. First, though, a word on how they developed. These 漢字 represent abstract concepts, so instead of developing from pictures, they are made up of a series of points and lines. You have learned other abstract 漢字, for example 力 (**power/strength**).

> ## Insight
> The 漢字 for strength 力 looks similar to the 漢字 for nine 九, so look carefully at the difference. There is also a picture to help you remember the difference: you bend your arm inwards to flex your muscle 力 whereas 九 has a Q-shape. Now look at the pictures.

Remembering the numbers 1

Here are some tips for remembering the 漢字 for numbers:

一、二、三 (1, 2, 3) These are easy – as you have probably noticed, they are composed of one, two and three lines.

四 This is a four-sided square and so is easy to relate to the number 4.

五 When you look at this 漢字, you can trace the arabic number 5 in it. Try it!

六 The number 6 in Japanese is pronunced roku – not unlike the English word rocket! With a little imagination, you should see a rocket taking off in this 漢字!

七 If you turn a continental number 7 upside down, this 漢字 emerges.

八 The arabic number 8 turned on its side is also the mathematical symbol for infinity. Imagine that the 漢字 is a road leading into the distance and on into infinity!

九 With a lot of imagination, this looks like a combination of the 漢字 for 8 and for 1, and of course 8 + 1 = 9.

十 The roman numeral for 10 is X. This looks like the 漢字 tilted to one side.

練習一 *Activity 1*

1 Match the sequence of 漢字 numbers on the left (a–f) with their equivalent sequences on the right (i–vi).

a 一、二、三、四   **i** 3, 6, 9

b 十、九、八、七   **ii** 2, 4, 6, 8

c 一、三、五、七   **iii** 8, 9, 10

d 三、六、九   **iv** 1, 2, 3, 4

e 二、四、六、八   **v** 1, 3, 5, 7

f 八、九、十   **vi** 10, 9, 8, 7

2 The following sequence of numbers 1–10 is out of order. Point at each of these 漢字 numbers in sequence then look back at the beginning of this section to check that you are correct.

三、五、六、一、九、八、二、十、四、七

3 Odd one out. The following sequences of 漢字 numbers all have one number missing when matched with the arabic numbers on the right. Which number is it?

a 一、二、三、四、五   1, 2, 3, 4, 5, 6

b 十、八、六、二   10, 8, 6, 4, 2

c 四、六、七、八   4, 5, 6, 7, 8

d 二、四、六、十   2, 4, 6, 8, 10

3.3 Numbers 11–99

These are easy to read because they are logically made from combinations of the 漢字 numbers 1–10. It is not necessary to write them all out for you, but here are the numbers 11–21 (in sequence) to give you an idea of how it works.

十一、十二、十三、十四、十五、十六、
十七、十八、十九、二十、二十一

Can you see the pattern? The numbers 11–19 are made up of 10 plus the relevant unit:

十一 = 10 + 1 = 11; 十二 = 10 + 2 = 12

20 is made up of a 2 in front of a 10: 二十. Remember the order like this: 2 + 10 (= 20). You then add the relevant unit to make 21, 22, 23, and so on:

二十一 = 2 + 10 + 1 = 21

二十二 = 2 + 10 + 2 = 22

二十三 = 2 + 10 + 3 = 23

練習二 *Activity 2*

1 The numbers 20, 30, 40, 50, 60, 70, 80, 90 follow in sequence. Look at them and make sure you can recognize them before moving on to the next activity.

二十、三十、四十、五十、六十、七十、
八十、九十

2 Now the same sequence has been jumbled up. Return the numbers to the original sequence by pointing at each in

turn. Then check with the previous sequence to see if you are right.

六十、九十、二十、四十、七十、五十、
三十、八十

3 How are you getting on so far? Remember you can always look back to earlier sections if you need to refresh your memory. Next, you are going to practise reading the sequence of numbers from 21–30. This time they have already been jumbled up. Can you put them in the correct sequence?

a 二十九   b 二十三   c 二十六   d 二十七
e 二十四   f 二十八   g 二十二   h 二十一
i 二十五   j 三十

Now check your answers at the back of the book.

4 Finally, you are going to pull together everything you have learned so far about numbers and have a go at reading a random selection of numbers between 1 and 99! Try writing down your answers in arabic numbers, then checking them at the back of the book. がんばって (ganbatte) – good luck!

a 九   b 六   c 七   d 十九
e 十七   f 十三   g 二十   h 五十
i 七十   j 二十一   k 三十二   l 四十三
m 五十四   n 六十五   o 七十六   p 八十七
q 八十八   r 九十九

How did you get on? You might find that this is a good place to take a break and digest what you have learned so far before moving on to the next section.

3.4 Five new kanji

Here are your five new 漢字:

百 100   千 1,000   万 10,000   円 yen
(Japanese currency) 年 year

Here are some visual clues and ideas to help you associate each 漢字 with its meaning:

百 (100)   Turned on its side, the 漢字 looks like this:

ᚺᔕ → ᚺᏲᏲ You can trace the numerals 100 in this.

千 (1,000)   This looks like the 漢字 for ten (十), but with an extra part on the top, in the same way that 1,000 looks like 10 but with two extra zeros!

万 (10,000)   If you look carefully at this, you can see a leaning **T** on the left and – ignoring the line at the top – you can also make out the shape of an **h**. Using a little twisted logic (!) you can let the **T** represent **ten** and the **Th** represent **thousand** – ten thousand!

Insight

In the Western counting system, we count in thousands until we reach one million. The Japanese system of counting is slightly different. Instead of saying two separate amounts – ten thousand – there is a specific word and 漢字 (万) to represent this amount.

To work out larger amounts of this unit, multiply the number by 10,000. For example:

十万 = 10 × 10,000 = 100,000
百万 = 100 × 10,000 = 1,000,000

円 The Japanese currency is the yen, represented by this 漢字 and by the international symbol ¥. All currencies can be written in words or numerals. For example: **six pounds** or **£6**, **six dollars** or **$6**, and in Japanese:

words: 六円　numerals: ¥6

The character 円, because it is a suffix to money amounts, is easy to recognize and remember.

年 Here is a visual image for remembering this 漢字:

Can you make out the left half of the 漢字 for **bamboo** (竹) at the front and a house shape behind? In Japan, bamboo decorations are put outside the front of houses at New Year, hence the visual clue leads you to the meaning **year**.

Look back over this section and remind yourself of the visual clues to the meanings, then try the next section.

練習三 *Activity 3*

1 Put these multiples of 100 into the correct order (100–900). Which one is missing?

a 九百	**b** 三百	**c** 五百	**d** 四百
e 百	**f** 二百	**g** 八百	**h** 七百

2 How do you write these 漢字 number amounts in arabic numbers?

a 八千	**b** 五千	**c** 七千	**d** 六千
e 二千	**f** 千 (or 一千)		

3 Match these multiples of 10,000 (a–e) with their arabic number equivalent (i–v).

a 二万　**b** 九万　**c** 九十万　**d** 百万　**e** 千万

i 90,000　　**ii** 1,000,000　　**iii** 20,000
iv 900,000　**v** 10,000,000

4 Combinations of 百、千、万

Put these amounts in order from the smallest to the largest.

a 二百　**b** 二千二百　**c** 二百万　**d** 二十万
e 二千　**f** 二千万　　**g** 二万

Now write out these amounts (in the new order) in arabic numbers.

5 Match the 漢字 money amounts (a–g) with their equivalent (i–vii).

a 三百円　　　　　　**i** ¥7,500

b 五千円　　　　　　**ii** ¥300

c 百五十円　　　　　**iii** ¥3,000

d 四百五十円　　　　**iv** ¥70,000

e 七万円　　　　　　**v** ¥5,000

f 七千五百円　　　　**vi** ¥450

g 三千円　　　　　　**vii** ¥150

3.5 More about dates

There are a number of ways in which the year can be written in Japanese. Let us look at these using the year 1999 as the model. Notice that the 漢字 for year (年) is written after the numbers.

1 千九百九十九年   This is 1999 written out in full using 漢字 numbers.

2 一九九九年   Here 1999 is written as it looks, 1–9–9–9.

3 1999年 ⎫
   99年 ⎭   The year is written in arabic numbers, notice that 年 is still used.

The first example is rarely used and the most commonly used is the third. Zero does not have a *kanji*, so is usually written as 0.

練習四 *Activity 4*

1 In this activity, you are going to match the years written in 漢字 (1–5) with those in arabic numerals (a–e).

1 一九六三年	**a** 2000 年
2 一八六三年	**b** 1963 年
3 二000年	**c** 1960 年
4 一六一六年	**d** 1616 年
5 一九六0年	**e** 1863 年

2 Now match the dates written in 漢字 (1–6) with those written in arabic (a–f).

1 十一月十一日	**a** 6月24日
2 六月十八日	**b** 3月31日
3 十月二日	**c** 6月18日
4 八月二十一日	**d** 11月11日
5 三月三十一日	**e** 8月21日
6 六月二十四日	**f** 10月2日

Dates are most often written with arabic numerals, but not always.

3 Now write out the dates 1–6 above in English.

3.6 The Japanese calendar

Used alongside the Western calendar in Japan is the Japanese system of 年号 (*nengō*) or **era names**. An era is defined by the length of rule of each Emperor. The present Emperor, Akihito, began his reign in 1989 and the new era is called 平成 (*Heisei*), which means **attainment of peace**. The previous era was called 昭和 (*Shōwa*), which means **enlightened peace**. Once an Emperor has died, he is referred to by the name of his era. Akihito's father, Hirohito, who died in 1989, is, therefore, now referred to as Emperor Shōwa. The 昭和 (*Shōwa*) era lasted for 63 years, from 1926–89.

Insight
The Japanese Emperor

The military powers controlling Japan before and during the Second World War used ancient historical documents which linked the Imperial line back to the sun goddess to promote and enforce the idea that the Emperor was divine and his word inviolable. At the end of the war, Emperor Hirohito publicly renounced this belief. In Japan's post-war constitution drawn up by the allies, the Emperor was reinstated only as a figurehead of the country. The current Emperor, Akihito, and his family are popular with the Japanese public, but war veterans from many western countries are still angry that there has never been an official apology from either Emperor or government for war crimes.

When the year is written according to the 年号 (*nengō*) system, it follows this pattern:

平成十一年 *Heisei* 11th year

To match this to the Western calendar, you count up from and including 1989, which was Heisei 1st year. Therefore:

平成十一年 = 1999

Arabic numbers can also be used: 平成 11 年

昭和 (*Shōwa*) years are counted from and including 1926. A good way of calculating these is to have an 'anchor' year – for example, your year of birth – then count from there:

昭和三十八年 (*Shōwa* 38th year) = 1963

Alternatively, add 25 years to the *Shōwa* year to get the Western year, or take 25 years away from the Western year to arrive at the *Shōwa* year:

昭和二十年 (*Shōwa* 20th year) = 20 + 25 = (19)45

1985 = 85 − 25 = 昭和六十年 (*Shōwa* 60th year)

Insight

A good way to work out the Western year since 2000 from the Heisei year is to take away 12 from the Heisei year to get the last two numbers of the Western year. Look at how this works:

平成二十二年 (Heisei 22nd year) → 22 − 12 = 10 → 2010

To do the reverse, isolate the last two numbers of the Western year and add 12:

2011 → 11 + 12 = 23 → 平成二十三年 (Heisei 23rd year)

練習五 *Activity 5*

1 Match the following 平成 (*Heisei*) years (a–f) with their Western calendar equivalents (i–vi).

a 平成四年	i 1994
b 平成十年	ii 1990
c 平成七年	iii 1997
d 平成六年	iv 1992
e 平成九年	v 1998
f 平成二年	vi 1995

The first year of an era is written not with 一 (one) but with 元 which means **beginning**:

平成元年 = Heisei 1st year (1989)

2 Match the following 昭和 (*Shōwa*) years (a–f) with their Western calendar equivalents (i–vi). Remember to add 25 years to the *Shōwa* year:

a 昭和四十八年	i 1939
b 昭和二十五年	ii 1926
c 昭和六十三年	iii 1973
d 昭和十四年	iv 1988
e 昭和四十三年	v 1950
f 昭和元年	vi 1968

3.7 読む練習三 Reading practice 3

This section will pull together everything you have learned in this unit and give you the opportunity to read numbers and dates in authentic contexts.

....

Insight

漢字 numbers are most often used when the text is written vertically (see Question 3 of Activity 6). Japanese business cards are often produced with the Japanese script written vertically on one side and the romanized script (for the benefit of non-Japanese clients) written horizontally on the other.

....

練習六 Activity 6

1 The following phone numbers are written horizontally. Notice that the area code is in brackets and a horizontal line (~) separates the two parts of the phone number. Do not confuse this with the number 一 (one). Can you convert them into arabic numerals?

a (0三) 　　三五八　　~ 一三七七

b (0九七) 　　五九二　　~ 四二一一

c (0七二0) 　　二一　　　~ 三八六六

d (0三) 　　三五九三　~ 二七0四

e (0二七九) 　　二二一　　~ 三一五四

2 The following is part of a newspaper advertisement for a series of three conferences. When will the conference be held (give the full date) in:

a London (ロンドン)?

b Tokyo (東京)?

c Dusseldorf (デュッセルドルフ)?

ロンドン '98年 12月 5日(土)
東京 '98年 12月 6日(日)
デュッセルドルフ '98年 12月12日(土)

3 The advertisement reproduced here is for a Japanese theatre production. Give the year, month, date and day of the performance in the Western calendar.

平成七年十月二十一日（土）

薪能

3.8 漢字の読み方 How to read kanji

In this section, you are going to focus on saying the numbers 1–10 in Japanese. If you have worked through *Get started in Japanese*, this is in Unit 2; in *Complete Japanese*, it is in Unit 1. Otherwise, turn to the 漢字 chart for Unit 3 at the back of this book and learn to say the onyomi reading for the numbers 1–10. Turn back to Section 2.8 in Unit 2 if you need to re-check the pronunciation rules.

Insight

Try memorizing how to say the numbers in Japanese by relating them to English-sounding words. For example, 一 (ichi) and 二 (ni) sound like itchy knee!

練習七 *Activity 7*

Align the numbers that follow with their 漢字 and *onyomi* reading. Check your answers against the Unit 3 漢字 chart at the back of the book.

漢字	英語 (*eigo*) English	音読み (*onyomi*)
三	one	SHICHI
五	two	KYŪ
六	three	NI
一	four	SHI
八	five	ICHI
九	six	HACHI
二	seven	JŪ
十	eight	ROKU
四	nine	GO
七	ten	SAN

3.9 書く練習三　Writing practice 3

In Units 1 and 2, you learned eight basic rules for writing 漢字 and you practised writing all the 漢字 you had learned in those units. Next, you are going to learn three simple rules for improving the shape of your strokes by looking at stroke endings. The Japanese learn calligraphy in order to perfect the shape of 漢字 using brushes, but if you pay attention to these three rules, you will be able to improve the way in which you write 漢字 even with a pen or pencil. The three main types of stroke ending are as follows:

1 STOP ending.
Your pen/pencil stops
and lifts off the page.

2 GRADUAL STOP.
You pull the pen gradually off the page with a sweeping motion.

3 FLICK.
The stroke flicks up at the end.

Now you are going to try writing the numbers 1–10 on squared paper (do not look at the stroke order that follows yet). Employ the eight rules you have learned and think about the stroke endings too from the previous examples.

Insight

The only exception is the number 9, where the vertical (left-hand) line is written first. This kanji has two strokes: you write the vertical first and then you write the second stroke across from the left, continue it down and across, then flick.

How did you get on? The numbers 1–10 follow, written out for you showing the stroke order. Look at the shapes and proportions of the strokes (for example, the left side of 8 is a different shape to the right side, and the same for 4 and 6; the strokes of 2 and 3 are not all the same length), then try to copy them as closely as possible.

3.10 終りに Conclusion

In this unit, you have been introduced to numbers up to 10,000 through 13 漢字. You have also learned the 漢字 for *yen* and for *year*. You have put this knowledge into practice to read number and money amounts, dates and telephone numbers. You have also learned about the Japanese calendar and have been introduced to two compound 漢字 words for the present and previous eras. Altogether, you have learned 15 single 漢字 (plus related compounds) and three new compound words (平成、昭和、年号). You have learned to count in Japanese from 1–10 and have applied the writing rules you learned previously to writing 漢字 numbers.

3.11 テスト Test yourself

How well can you recognize Japanese numbers and their function? Look at these numbers. Can you change them into arabic numbers and identify their function (i.e. a date, a phone number or an amount of money)?

1 四万五千二百円

2 平成二十一年

3 0三　五六二　一九八九

4 三月二十六日

5 二00八年

6 昭和六十二年

4

....

第四課
Unit 4

In this unit, you will:
- *learn to recognize 12 漢字 used in action words (verbs)*
- *be introduced to words made up of combinations of these and other 漢字*
- *learn more about pronouncing and writing 漢字*

4.1 はじめに Introduction

In Unit 2, you learned that some 漢字, as well as having meanings in themselves, are used as components of more complex 漢字 (see Section 2.4). The 漢字 you will be introduced to in this lesson are created from simpler 漢字, some of which you have learned already. In the following activity, you are going to review some key 漢字 to refresh your memory before moving on to learning the new 漢字 in this unit.

1 Can you remember the meanings of these 漢字?

a 口　b 耳　c 人　d 目　e 山
f 門　g 木　h 日　i 子

2 Now look at the following new 漢字. They each contain simple 漢字 as part of their structure. Can you spot them? (You do not need to know the meaning of the whole 漢字 at this stage.)

a 聞	**b** 見	**c** 書	**d** 言
e 学	**f** 買	**g** 休	**h** 出

Check the answers to these two activities in the back before moving on to the next section.

4.2 Finding clues

The new 漢字 introduced in the second activity you have just completed can all be used as verbs (that is, action or doing words – words you can put I, **you, he/she** etc. in front of). So far, you have not learned the meaning of any of them, but you have identified simpler 漢字 within them. These can be a clue to their meanings, and you are going to use these clues to work out the meanings for yourself. Before you can do this, here are three extra pieces of information.

1 This shape 儿 ( ) when used as a 漢字 component has the meaning **human legs**. You can see it in 2b of the Introduction above.

2 This shape 八 ( ) has the meaning **animal legs**. You can see it in 2f.

3 The 漢字 for person (人) takes this form when used as part of a more complex 漢字. You can see an example of this in 2g.

練習一 *Activity 1*

The following seven 漢字 (a–g) all represent verbs. The story clues (1–7) link the different components of each 漢字 into a story which indicates the 漢字 meaning. (The component meanings are in **bold**.) This technique should help you to remember that meaning. Can you work out which 漢字 has which meaning?

a 聞 **b** 見 **c** 言 **d** 学 **e** 買 **f** 休 **g** 出

Story clues

1 A **person** resting by a **tree** during their work break.
Meaning: **to rest; holiday**

2 An **eye** running around on **human legs**.
Meaning: **to look, watch, see**

3 **Mountains** upon **mountains**, but somewhere there is a way out.
Meaning: **to go out**

4 A neighbour is pressing an **ear** between the **gates** of the house to hear the gossip.
Meaning: **to hear, listen**

5 An **eye** with **animal legs** is a shellfish. A sideways **eye** above it is a human inspecting it before buying.
Meaning: **to buy**

6 At school, the **child** is expected to wear a special **hat** when studying.
Meaning: to study

7 The **mouth** spoke words which rose up in **lines**.
Meaning: to say; words

How did you get on? Here are the same 漢字, this time with their meanings and a picture representation as well:

ear at the gates.
聞 to listen, to hear

Let's go to see!
=3 見 to see, watch, look

言 to say
blah blah ...

学 to study

休 to rest

I'll have this, please.
買 to buy

Way Out
出 to go out

Now read through the stories again. Do you see how the components of these 漢字 help to indicate their meanings?

練習二 *Activity 2*

This is a quick activity designed to help you review the 漢字 learned so far in this unit. Simply match the 漢字 on the left (1–7) with the meanings on the right (a–g).

1 買   **a** to listen

2 休   **b** to look

3 出	**c** to say
4 聞	**d** to study
5 学	**e** to go out
6 見	**f** to buy
7 言	**g** to rest

練習三 *Activity 3*

Here are the next seven 漢字 which you will learn in this unit:

売　読　話　書　食　飲　入

Some of the components which make up these 漢字 are contained in the following list. Can you locate and ring the appropriate part on the 漢字 above? The number in brackets indicates the number of times the component appears.

1 儿 human legs (+2)
2 言 to say (+2)
3 口 mouth (+3)
4 土 earth (+2)
5 日 sun (+1)
6 千 1,000 (+1)

How did you get on? You can find the answers in the sections that follow.

4.3 More kanji components

The handwritten 漢字 which follow have had their component parts numbered. These numbers are referred to in the explanations. A story is given to help you remember the meaning.

Kanji A

1 This upper part looks like 土 (**earth**), except that the top horizontal line is longer, like this: 士. In fact, this 漢字 means **samurai**, but when used as part of a more complex 漢字, we are going to take its meaning as **earth**.
2 In between the legs and the earth is a table.
3 'Human legs'.

Story: **People walked** over to the **tabletop** sale to see a **samurai** selling clods of **earth**.
Meaning: to sell 売

Kanji B

1 You should have identified **to say/words** (言) at the left of this 漢字.
2 Can you see that this is the same as the 漢字 you have just learned (**to sell** 売)?

Story: Notice outside a bookstore: '**Words for sale**. Buy a book and read the **words**.'
Meaning: to read 読

Kanji C

1 Once again, the left side is **to say/words**.
2 1,000 (千).
3 **mouth** (口). Together, **2** and **3** make up the 漢字 for **tongue** (舌).

Story: **Thousands** of **words** were spoken by the **tongue**.
Meaning: **to talk, speak** 話

Kanji D

1 This comes from a 漢字 you have not learned yet, **brush** (筆). Before pens were invented, writing was done with calligraphy brushes. Here is a picture to help you link the meaning to the character:

2 You should have recognized this as **sun**. An alternative meaning is **mouth** (口) with a line in it (日). You could think of this as a condensed version of 言 (**to say**) with the words about to come out of the mouth.

Story: Written **words** are created by a **calligraphy brush**.
Meaning: **to write** 書

Kanji E

1 Think of this as a roof, in this case, the roof of a house.
2 This means **white** and represents the sun with a ray coming off it. In ancient China, the rays of the sun were seen as white.
3 This lower part is actually a truncated version of 火 (**fire**), which you learned in Unit 1.

Story: **White** rice boiled over a **fire** in a Japanese home.
Meaning: **to eat; food** 食

Kanji F

1 You have just been introduced to the left side of this 漢字. It is slightly truncated, but indicates the same meaning – **food**.
2 A more detailed picture of the right side will help you with the meaning.

Story: The left side gives the general meaning (**food**). The right side is a person taking a drink.
Meaning: **to drink; a drink** 飲

Kanji G

In this new 漢字, the 'person' appears to be walking back across the page. The printed version 入 shows this 'person' clearly indicating their direction (flick at the top points to the left).

Story: **People** going in walk to the **left**.
Meaning: to enter, go in 入

> **Insight**
>
> Notice the difference between the handwritten and printed
> versions (入) of this 漢字. And do not confuse it with the
> kanji for person (printed = 人; handwritten = 人).

練習四 *Activity 4*

This is a review activity for you to test yourself on the second set of 漢字 you have just learned. Match the 漢字 on the left (1–7) with the meanings on the right (a–g).

1 食   **a** drink
2 入   **b** eat
3 売   **c** read
4 書   **d** talk
5 飲   **e** enter
6 話   **f** sell
7 読   **g** write

How did you get on? If you are still uncertain about some of these, read through the stories and look at the composition of each 漢字 again, until you are sure.

4.4 読む練習四 Reading practice 4

You now know the first 漢字 of the instruction in this heading – it means **read**. Before you try this next section, let us summarize the 漢字 you have learned in this unit. First, look at the 漢字 and see if you can remember the meaning before looking at the corresponding English translations below.

1 聞	**2** 見	**3** 書	**4** 言
5 学	**6** 買	**7** 休	**8** 出
9 売	**10** 読	**11** 話	**12** 食
13 飲	**14** 入		

1 listen	**2** look	**3** write	**4** say
5 study	**6** buy	**7** rest	**8** go out
9 sell	**10** read	**11** speak	**12** eat
13 drink	**14** enter		

練習五 *Activity 5*

Here are some sentences in Japanese (1–7) followed by their English translations (a–g). At this stage, you will not be able to read the whole sentence, because you have not learned *hiragana* yet (Unit 5). There is also one 漢字 (語)* which you have not seen yet. However, you will be able to understand the key words of the sentence from your knowledge of 漢字. By matching these with the full English sentences, you will be able to get the meaning of the whole sentence. The 漢字 you have already learned have numbers below them. These refer to the unit in which the 漢字 was first introduced so that you can check back if you need to. For example:

男の人は車を買いました。　*The man (male person)*
2　　2　　2　　4　　　　*bought a car.*

Now have a go yourself. Match each sentence to its English
translation.

がんばって! *ganbatte!* Good luck!

1 女　人は　　　　日本語*を　　　学びました。
　　2　2　　　　　1　2 (7)　　　4
2 女の子は　　　　土曜日に　　　休みました。
　　2　2　　　　　1　　　　　4
3 男の人は　　　　月を　　　　　見ました。
　　2　2　　　　　1　　　　　4
4 林さんは　　　　森田さんに　　話しました。
　　2　　　　　　1　2　　　　4
5 男の子は　　　　馬が　　　　　好きです。
　　2　2　　　　　2　　　　　2
6 女の人は　　　　竹の子を　　　食べました。
　　2　2　　　　　1　2　　　　4
7 山田さんは　　　車を　　　　　売りました。
　　2 1　　　　　2　　　　　4

a The woman (female person) ate some bamboo shoots (bamboo
children). (*lit.* The woman some bamboo shoots ate.)
b The girl (female child) rested on Saturday. (*lit.* The girl on
Saturday rested.)

c Mr Yamada (Mountain-rice field) sold his car. (*lit*. Mr Yamada his car sold.)

d The boy (male child) likes horses. (*lit*. The boy horses likes.)

e The woman (female person) studied Japanese. (*lit*. The woman Japanese studied.)

f Mr Hayashi (Wood) talked to Mrs Morita (Forest-rice field). (*lit*. Mr Hayashi to Mrs Morita talked.)

g The man (male person) looked at the moon. (*lit*. The man at the moon looked.)

How did you get on? Check your answers at the back of the book.

4.5 More kanji compounds

In this section, you will be introduced to some new compound 漢字 words. First, you need to learn a new 漢字:

物 **thing**

This 漢字 is used to make verbs into nouns. This is best explained with an example:

買 (**to buy**) + 物 (**thing**) = 買物 = **shopping** (*lit*. buying things)

練習六 *Activity 6*

The 漢字 compounds that follow have been made into nouns by adding 物 (**thing**) to them. Can you work out what their meanings would be in English? There is a list of English words in random order on the next page which you can refer to if you need to.

1 飲物   **2** 食物   **3** 売物

4 見物   **5** 書物   **6** 読物

a writing	**b** food	**c** items for sale
d sightseeing	**e** book	**f** drinks

練習七 *Activity 7*

Here are some more compound words (1–7) using 漢字
you have been introduced to in this unit. See if you can work
out their meanings by matching them with their English
equivalents (a–g).

1 売買		**a** a study visit
2 読書		**b** start school
3 入学		**c** eating and drinking
4 出入		**d** absence from school (long term)
5 飲食		**e** reading
6 見学		**f** buying and selling
7 休学		**g** going in and out

練習八 *Activity 8*

This activity introduces compound 漢字 words which use
漢字 from the first four units of this book. Think about the
literal meaning, then see if you can work out what you would
say in English. The box of English words (in random order)
will act as a checklist once you think you have worked out
the meaning of a word. Here are some amusing examples to get
you started!

例 *Rei* 1 出目金 *lit.* go out eye gold = **a pop-eyed goldfish**
例 *Rei* 2 休火山 *lit.* resting fire mountain = **a dormant volcano**
例 *Rei* 3 二足 *lit.* two feet = **two pairs (of footwear)**

1 売人	**2** 入口	**3** 出口	**4** 飲水
5 学力	**6** 買手	**7** 休日	**8** 日本人

4.6 漢字の読み方 How to read kanji

You were first introduced to how 漢字 are pronounced in Unit 2 and
you can refer back to that unit for guidance on pronunciation. In this
section in Unit 3, you used the *kanji* chart at the back of the book to
learn the *onyomi* (Chinese readings) of the numbers 1–10. Now turn
to the chart for Unit 4 at the back of the book which contains all the
single 漢字 introduced in this unit. Focus on the *onyomi* readings and
try to memorize them. Here are some hints to help you.

Insight
Ways of remembering how to read kanji

1 Look back at the simple pronunciation rules you were
   given in Unit 2.

2 Say the readings out loud.

3 See if you can match each reading to an English word and
   make a little story to help you remember. For example,
   the *onyomi* of 食 (eat) is *SHOKU*. So how about: 'It was a
   SHOCK how much food he could eat!' And the onyomi of 見
   (look) is *KEN* so: '*KEN* looked out of the window.'
   Do you get the idea?

4 Test yourself by covering up the reading, looking at the 漢
   字 and saying the reading out loud.

練習九 Activity 9

1 This is a simple linking activity. Link the 漢字 (1–14) with their
   correct reading (a–m).

   1 買   **a** *DOKU*

   2 休   **b** *SHOKU*

3	出	**c** *NYŪ*
4	聞	**d** *BAI (use twice)*
5	学	**e** *KYŪ*
6	見	**f** *SHUTSU*
7	言	**g** *WA*
8	食	**h** *BUN*
9	入	**i** *KEN*
10	売	**j** *IN*
11	飲	**k** *GAKU*
12	話	**l** *SHO*
13	書	**m** *GEN*
14	読	

2 Now try saying these compound 漢字 words in Japanese.

a 売買 (buying and selling)
b 読書 (reading)
c 入学 (start school)
d 出入 (going in and out)
e 飲食 (eating and drinking)
f 見学 (study visit)
g 休学 (absence from school)
h 見聞 (knowledge; experience)

4.7 書く練習四 Writing practice 4

You should now recognize the first 漢字 in this heading – it means *write*. In this section, you are going to learn to write the 14 漢字 which have been introduced in this unit.

Insight

- Remember: stroke order is important for writing accurately, for helping you to remember the 漢字 and for counting the number of strokes. And there are sometimes slight differences between handwritten and printed versions of the same 漢字.

- One way to remember how to write more complex 漢字 is to visualize the components they are made up of. For example, in preparing yourself to write 聞 (listen) from memory, say to yourself 'gate and ear'. Look carefully at the proportions and overall balance of each 漢字. For example, where a 漢字 has a distinct left and right side, the left side is narrower (the proportions are approximately left side = 1/3; right side = 2/3).

| 聞 | 聞 |

| 門 | 門 | 門 | 門 |

| 門 | 門 | 聞 |

| 学 | 学 |

| 丶 | ﾂ | ﾂ | ﾂ |

| ﾝ | 学 | 学 | 学 |

| 見 | 見 | 目 | 貝 | 見 |

| 言 | 言 |

| 丶 | 亠 | 亠 | 言 | 言 |

4.8 終りに Conclusion

In this unit, you have been introduced to 14 漢字 which represent action words and have learned to pronounce their onyomi and to write them. You have also learned the meanings of 26 compound 漢字 words and have identified the key words in a set of Japanese sentences. Now try the test to see how well you have remembered the 漢字 you have learned in the first four units!

4.9 テスト Test yourself

The 漢字 (including some compound words) you have learned so far are grouped in themes. Can you remember their English meanings? (Some 漢字 appear more than once if they cover more than one category.)

1 People and animals

    a 馬　　**b** 人　　**c** 女　　**d** 男
    e 子　　**f** 女子　　**g** 男子　　**h** 日本人

2 Elements of nature

    a 山　　**b** 火山　　**c** 川　　**d** 水　　**e** 火
    f 木　　**g** 林　　**h** 森　　**i** 田

3 Numbers and money

    a 一　　**b** 五　　**c** 六十円　　**d** 百
    e 四千円　　**f** 二万　　**g** 金　　**h** 三千七百

4 Dates

    a 九月十一日 (土)　　**b** 八月二十日
    c 一九九一年　　**d** 平成十二年

5 Verbs (action words)

| a | 聞 | b | 食 | c | 飲 | d | 言 | e | 話 |
| f | 読 | g | 売 | h | 見 | i | 買 | j | 休 |

6 Parts of the body

| a | 耳 | b | 口 | c | 足 | d | 目 | e | 手 |

5

....

第五課
Unit 5

In this unit, you will:

- *learn to read the 46 ひらがな (hiragana) symbols which make up the phonetic 'alphabet'*
- *learn some rules for making extra sounds from the 46 main symbols*
- *be introduced to picture–sound associations to make learning easier*
- *learn how to write ひらがな (hiragana)*
- *have a go at reading some words and phrases*

5.1 はじめに Introduction

Look back to **Only got five minutes?** at the start of this book and read the overview of the different types of Japanese script, in particular the section on ひらがな (*hiragana*). Then answer the following questions based on the information you have just read.

1 What are the two main uses of ひらがな?
2 Which script (漢字、ひらがな、カタカナ (*katakana*)) is learned first by Japanese children in primary schools?
3 What did ひらがな develop from?
4 How many basic symbols make up the modern ひらがな syllabary?

5.2 Work it out!

You have not learned to read any ひらがな yet (apart from these four symbols), but try this simple matching activity. There are six ひらがな words (a–f) in the left column which are repeated in a different order in the right column. Match up the same words and write the correct letter in the brackets. The first one is done for you.

a すし   つくえ ( )
b あき   せいと ( )
c こえ   すし **(a)**
d つくえ   こえ ( )
e さとう   あき ( )
f せいと   さとう ( )

5.3 How to read hiragana

Let us begin by looking at the first four lines of the ひらがな syllabary with the romanized pronunciation and learn how to read them.

Insight

Notice that the chart is written in the traditional way, from top to bottom and from right to left. Therefore, you read in columns rather than rows. And you begin to read from the top right-hand corner.

ta た	sa さ	ka か	a あ
chi ち	shi し	ki き	i い
tsu つ	su す	ku く	u う
te て	se せ	ke け	e え
to と	so そ	ko こ	o お

Can you now answer these two questions?

1 What is the first ひらがな symbol?
2 Which column do you read first, and in what order?

To save you looking in the back, the answers are 1 あ a

2 あ a、い i、う u、え e、お o.

The next point to notice is that the first five sounds are what we call vowel sounds. In Unit 2 (Section 2.8), you were introduced to the pronunciation of Japanese sounds.

Insight

Here is a quick checklist to help you remember the pronunciation.

あ	a	as in mat		え	e	as in end
い	i	as in hit		お	o	as in hot
う	u	as in blue				

And, as you also learned in Unit 2, consonants are attached to each of these vowels to create new sounds. Each of these sounds is represented by a ひらがな symbol. This is why the Japanese syllabary is called 'a phonetic alphabet'.

Insight

The difference in the way the Japanese syllabary and our roman alphabet work is that whereas the roman alphabet consists of 26 letters which are used in various combinations to create a wide range of sounds, with the Japanese system the sounds have already been 'created', and every symbol represents one of these sounds. This makes spelling very easy, because the sounds are constant, unlike English, in which you cannot look at a word and know for sure how each letter is pronounced until you have learned complex spelling and sound rules. For example, think of the **a** sound in mat, mate, mayor and major.

練習一 *Activity 1*

In the Work it out! activity in this unit (Section 5.2), you matched six ひらがな words. This time, you are going to try to read these words. Use the chart of the first 20 symbols that follows and see if you can say the words. Their English meanings are given in brackets.

a すし (sushi)
b あき (autumn)
c こえ (voice)
d つくえ (desk)
e さとう (sugar)
f せいと (school pupil)

5.4 The hiragana chart

On the following pages, you are going to be introduced to the whole ひらがな chart, including the correct order to write each symbol. To help you understand the layout of the chart, an explanation is now given using the first symbol あ.

The printed version of each symbol is also included (top left-hand corner) because this sometimes differs slightly from the handwritten version.

80

な na	た ta	さ sa	か ka	あ a
な	た	さ	か	あ
ー ナ ナ な	ー ナ た た	ー さ さ	つ カ か	ー さ あ
に ni	ち chi	し shi	き ki	い i
に	ち	し	き	い
／ に に	ー ち	し	ー ニ キ き	／ い
ぬ nu	つ tsu	す su	く ku	う u
ぬ	つ	す	く	う
／ ぬ	つ	ー す	く	` う
ね ne	て te	せ se	け ke	え e
ね	て	せ	け	え
／ ね	て	ー ナ せ	／ ／ け	` え
の no	と to	そ so	こ ko	お o
の	と	そ	こ	お
の	＼ と	` そ	ー こ	ー お お

Insight

Have a go at writing the ひらがな because this will help you to remember how to read them. The basic rules you learned for 漢字 also apply here – you write horizontal strokes from left to right, and vertical/diagonal strokes from top to bottom. As you write each one (using graph paper if possible), say its sound to yourself.

練習二 *Activity 2*

The activities in this unit will keep referring you back to the different charts, so do not worry about learning all the symbols at once! There is also a section later to help you explore ways to remember the 46 basic ひらがな symbols, but first here is an activity to get you reading.

わ wa	ら ra	や ya	ま ma	は ha
わ	ら	や	ま	は
	り ri		み mi	ひ hi
	り		み	ひ
を wo	る ru	ゆ yu	む mu	ふ fu
を	る	ゆ	む	ふ
	れ re		め me	へ he
	れ		め	へ
ん n	ろ ro	よ yo	も mo	ほ ho
ん	ろ	よ	も	ほ

Each sequence of ひらがな symbols in the activity is taken from a column, row or diagonal of the chart. Try to read (out loud) each of the ひらがな, then refer back to the relevant part of the chart to refresh your memory. Then try again to read the sequence from memory. Continue like this until you can read the sequence confidently, then move on to the next one. Keep an eye on the printed version to get used to these too.

The first part of this activity refers to the first page of the chart.

82

1 The third column (always count from the right): さ、し、す、せ、そ

2 The third row (reading from right to left): う、く、す、つ、ぬ

3 The diagonal from top left to bottom right: な、ち、す、け、お

4 The diagonal from top right to bottom left: あ、き、す、て、の

5 The second column: か、き、く、け、こ

6 The fourth row: え、け、せ、て、ね

Insight

Have you noticed that the syllables in the row sequences always end with the same vowel sound? The only exceptions in the charts in this book are を (wo) and ん (n) – を (wo) would normally be in the o ending row and ん (n) would have its column. Their positions in this chart are purely so that they fit on the page. By the way, を is transliterated as wo to distinguish it from お (o). It is used as a grammatical marker, whereas お (o) is used to form words.

Now look at the sequences 1–6 again and answer these questions.

7 How many times do the symbols **a** し **b** き **c** て appear?
8 Which symbol appears three times?
9 Which symbol appears the most times?

(Answers to 7–9 are at the back of the book.)

The second part of this activity refers to the second page of the chart.

10 The first column: は、ひ、ふ、へ、ほ
11 The fourth column: ら、り、る、れ、ろ

12 The fifth row: ほ、も、よ、ろ、ん

13 The diagonal from top left to bottom right: わ、り、
ゆ、め、ほ

14 The diagonal from top right to bottom left: は、み、
ゆ、れ、ん

Now look at the sequences 10–14 again and answer these
questions.

15 How often do the symbols **a** れ and **b** ん appear?
16 How many symbols only appear once?
17 Which symbol appears the most times?

(Answers to 15–17 are at the back of the book.)

....

Insight
Remembering hiragana

One way of remembering ひらがな is through visual
and sound association (mnemonics). The basic idea is that
you find a way to make the shape of each symbol suggest a
picture or story which connects it to its sound.

Here are some ideas for remembering the first five ひらが
な. Concentrate on the sounds (for example, aim = e) rather
than the letters or spellings.

....

1 (*a*)   **2** (*i*)   **3** (*u*)   **4** (*e*)   **5** (*o*)

Stories

1 あ (*a*) is an opera singer singing an _aria_ (Japanese pronunciation has a short 'a' sound)

2 い (*i*) is an American _Indian_   **4** え (*e*) _aim_ for the target

3 う (*u*) _ooh_, my back hurts!   **5** お (*o*) is an _ostrich_

Do you get the idea? Here are another ten to get you started. If you find this method helps you, try to think of your own. You might not have inspiration for all of them at first, but try a few at a time and write down your ideas in a notebook.

1   **2**   **3**   **4**   **5**

6   **7**   **8**   **9**   **10**

Stories

1 ひ (*hi*) is someone laughing, _hee_ hee

2 わ (*wa*) is a baby crying, _waaaa_

3 く (*ku*) for _cuck_oo

4 と (*to*) is the _toe_ of a shoe

5 ね (*ne*) is the Loch _Ness_ monster

6 ち (*chi*) is a _cheer_leader

7 ぬ (*nu*) looks like a bowl of _noodles_

8 し (*shi*) _she's_ got long hair

9 け (*ke*) for _KO_ (knocked out)

10 こ (*ko*) is a _Cox_ apple

練習三 *Activity 3*

Now that you have been introduced to the 46 ひらがな symbols, it is time to put your learning into practice and try reading some words. To make it easier for you, the words are in three sets. Set 1 consists of ひらがな from the first page of the chart and Set 2 consists of those from the second page. The final challenge is Set 3, which comprises words using ひらがな from the whole chart. See how many symbols/words you can read from memory, then use the chart to search for those you cannot remember. Where you have already learned the 漢字 for a word, this is also given in brackets. However, the purpose of this activity is to practise reading ひらがな.

Set 1

a あさ (morning)　**b** て (hand 手)　**c** なつ (summer)

d とけい (clock)　**e** しお (salt)　**f** なに (what)

g ぬの (cloth)

Set 2

a よる (evening)　　　**b** みみ (ear 耳)

c はる (spring)　　　**d** ふゆ (winter)

e むら (village)　　　**f** やま (mountain 山)

g もり (forest 森)　　　**h** わん (bowl)

Set 3

a おはよう (good morning)　**b** さようなら (goodbye)

c ねこ (cat) **d** せんせい (teacher)
e いぬ (dog) **f** め (eye 目)
g へそ (navel) **h** ひと (person 人)
i れい (example 例) **j** にほん (Japan 日本)

Insight
Keep coming back to this activity. Try keeping a score of how many words you can read each time and challenge yourself to improve it!

Similar hiragana

You have probably confused some of the similar-looking ひらがな already. This section will line these up and point out the differences to help you keep them separate in your mind.

Insight
Notice the punctuation – a comma 、 and a full stop 。 – not all that different from English.

き、さ。	き (ki) has two horizontal lines, さ (sa) has one.
さ、ち。	さ (sa) leans to the left, ち (chi) looks like the number 5 (the top has slipped!)
い、こ。	い (i) is more or less vertical, こ (ko) is horizontal.
い、り。	い (i) – the left stroke is slightly longer than the right, り (ri) – the right stroke is longer than the left (hand written version).
け、は、ほ。	け (ke) has no loop at the end, は (ha) has only one horizontal line, ほ (ho) has two horizontal lines.

ほ、ま。	The top horizontal line in ほ (ho) sits on top of the vertical line whereas in ま (ma) both horizontal lines cut through the vertical.
す、む。	す (su) curves to the left, む (mu) curves to the right and has an extra stroke flick.
ぬ、め、ね。	ぬ (nu) has two stroke ends at the top and a loop at the bottom whereas め (me) has the same stroke ends but no loop, and ね (ne) has only one vertical stroke.
る、ろ。	る (ru) has a loop, ろ (ro) looks a bit like a number 3.

5.5 Contracted sounds

You have now been introduced to the 46 basic ひらがな symbols. As well as these 46, there are other sounds which are made by combining some of the basic symbols. This is done by combining the symbols which end in the i sound (き、し、ち、に、ひ、み、り) with a small version of や、ゆ、or よ。Each sound is pronounced as a single syllable or 'beat'. Look at the following chart:

き (ki) → きや (kya)　きゆ (kyu)　きよ (kyo)
し (shi) → しや (sha)　しゆ (shu)　しよ (sho)
ち (chi) → ちや (cha)　ちゆ (chu)　ちよ (cho)
に (ni) → にや (nya)　にゆ (nyu)　によ (nyo)
ひ (hi) → ひや (hya)　ひゆ (hyu)　ひよ (hyo)
み (mi) → みや (mya)　みゆ (myu)　みよ (myo)
り (ri) → りや (rya)　りゆ (ryu)　りよ (ryo)

練習四 *Activity 4*

This activity is going to utilize some of the wide range of onomatopoeic words which the Japanese have in their language. These are words which sound like the action or sound word they name.

Insight

- In Japanese, onomatopoeic words usually repeat a sound twice. The nearest English equivalents are phrases such as woof woof for a dog's bark; plip plop for the sound of rain and gobble gobble for the sound of a turkey, but words like this in Japanese are not limited to children's words.

- One point to note before you start this activity – many of the words that follow are lengthened by the addition of a vowel sound, normally う (u), at the end (but あ (a) is also used in these examples). For instance, ちゅうちゅう (a mouse's squeak) is pronounced chuu chuu (usually written chū chū – the line over the vowel represents the additional u). Let one sound run into the other smoothly – do not separate ちゅ (chu) and う (u).

Now practise reading and saying the following onomatopoeic words. Refer back to the earlier chart to help you as necessary. Two symbols you have learned previously, ん (n) and ろ (ro) are also used here.

a きゃあきゃあ (scream with laughter)
b しゅんしゅん (fizzing sound)
c しゅうしゅう (fizzing sound)
d ちゅうちゅう (mouse's squeak)
e にゃあにゃあ (miaow)
f ひゅうひゅう (whistling sound)

g ひよろ　ひよろ (swaying; lanky)

h きよろ　きよろ (looking around)

5.6 Hiragana that change their sound

> **Insight**
>
> You have learned nearly all the extra rules for ひらがな,
> so you can relax, they are not endless! Also, if you think you
> have taken in enough at any stage, leave this unit, carry on
> with the 漢字 units and come back to this later. You are not
> expected to remember everything in this unit in one go, and
> no one is setting the pace except you!

Some of the ひらがな symbols change their sound with the
addition of two small strokes ゛ *(ten ten)* at the top right of the
symbol. Let us look at these.

1 k sounds become g sounds (hard *g* as in **get**):

か、き、く、け、こ → が、ぎ、ぐ、げ、ご
(ka, ki, ku, ke, ko)　　 ga　 gi　 gu　 ge　 go

2 s sounds → z sounds:

さ、し、す、せ、そ → ざ、じ、ず、ぜ、ぞ
(sa, shi, su, se, so)　　 za　 ji　 zu　 ze　 zo*

　*じ is pronounced ji.

3 t sounds become d sounds:

た、ち、つ、て、と → だ、(ぢ づ)、で、ど
(ta, chi, tsu, te, to)　　 da　 (ji　 zu)　 de　 do

Insight

The sounds ぢ (ji) and づ (zu) are not normally used because they create the same sound as じ (ji) and ず (zu). See 2.

4 h sounds become b sounds:

は、 ひ、 ふ、 へ、 ほ → ば、 び、 ぶ、 べ、 ぼ
(*ha,   hi,   fu,   he,   ho*)   *ba   bi   bu   be   bo*

5 In addition, h sounds become p sounds when a small circle (*maru*) is added:

は、 ひ、 ふ、 へ、 ほ → ぱ、 ぴ、 ぷ、 ぺ、 ぽ
(*ha,   hi,   fu,   he,   ho*)   *pa   pi   pu   pe   po*

These five sets of rules cover all the sound changes for single ひらがな symbols. Look over these rules, cover up the *rōmaji* and try reading them, then try the simple activity that follows.

練習五 *Activity 5*

Say the sounds out loud or write them down. Refer to the rules given earlier for the answers.

a ぎ、 じ、 び、 ぴ　　**b** げ、 ぜ、 で、 べ、 ぺ
c が、 ざ、 だ、 ば、 ぱ　**d** ぐ、 ず、 ぶ、 ぷ
e ご、 ぞ、 ど、 ぼ、 ぽ

Finally, do you remember the contracted sounds you learned in Section 5.5? Well, the rules just given also apply to these. The chart that follows groups these sounds on the left. The *rōmaji* is also given on the right but cover this up and see if you can work out how to read the ひらがな before you refer to the *rōmaji*.

ぎゃ、ぎゅ、ぎょ	*gya, gyu, gyo*
じゃ、じゅ、じょ	*ja, ju, jo*
びゃ、びゅ、びょ	*bya, byu, byo*
ぴゃ、ぴゅ、ぴょ	*pya, pyu, pyo*

5.7 The small つ (tsu)

The final rule you need to know in order to read ひらがな
properly is the use of the small つ in a word. When you see this,
you do not pronounce it but pause slightly (a glottal stop) before
saying the next sound.

Insight

The small つ (*tsu*) is shown in *rōmaji* by doubling the next
consonant. The length of this pause is the same as in these
English examples: *headdress* (pause after 'hea'; the first *d* is
not pronounced); and *bookcase* (pause after 'boo').

Here are some Japanese examples with the *rōmaji* and a
pronunciation guide beneath:

a まって (*wait!*) **b** きって (*stamp*) **c** きっぷ (*ticket*)
matte   *kitte*   *kippu*
ma (pause) *te*   *ki* (pause) *te*   *ki* (pause) *pu*

5.8 読む練習五 Reading practice 5

Take a deep breath! You are now going to put into practice
everything you have learned in this unit. These initial activities
will keep referring you back to the different sections and
remember – you can keep revisiting these activities to see if you

can improve your score. You do not need to be perfect first time round! Most of these words are usually written with 漢字, but the purpose of the activities that follow is to practise reading ひらがな.

練習六　*Activity 6*

This activity will use ひらがな from the initial chart (Section 5.4) and contracted sounds (Section 5.5).

See how many of these words you can read.

a きゃく (customer)

b きよう (today)

c ぎゅうにゅう (milk)

d しゃしん (photograph)

e じゃね (See you!)

f ちょうしょく (breakfast)

g ちゅうしょく (lunch)

h ひゃく (100)

i びょういん (hospital)

j りょこう (travel)

練習七　*Activity 7*

This activity will use ひらがな from the initial chart (Section 5.4) plus ひらがな which change their sound (Section 5.6). Once again, see how many of these words you can read.

a みず (water)

b かぎ (keys)

c じてん (dictionary)

d でんわ (telephone)

e たんぽぽ (dandelion)

f どきどき (sound of heart beating fast)

g がぶがぶ (gulping sound – when drinking)

練習八 *Activity 8*

This activity gives you practice at reading words with the small つ (Section 5.7).

a ちよっと (a little)   **b** まって (wait)
c やっぱり (as expected)   **d** がっこう (school)
e がんばって (Good luck!)   **f** まっすぐ (straight
                                    ahead)

5.9 Hiragana and kanji

You will already have noticed from the instruction words used throughout this book (and in the last activity) that Japanese is written as a mixture of ひらがな and 漢字 (and カタカナ – *katakana*, introduced in Unit 9). The ひらがな parts of the words have a grammatical function. As mentioned in the **Introduction**, Japanese children first learn to read and write using only ひらがな. As they learn 漢字, they make their writing more sophisticated by replacing words and parts of words written in ひらがな with 漢字.

Insight

Although it may seem to be a simpler task to read using ひらがな (rather than having to learn 2,000 漢字!), in fact, once you know 漢字, texts become easier to read and scan because 漢字 offer visual clues to the meaning.

練習九 *Activity 9*

You have learned that ひらがな has a grammatical function. Now you are going to put this to practice. Below are five of the verbs (action words) you learned in Unit 4. (For those of you who have *Get started in Japanese*, verbs are introduced in Unit 8.) Here are the points to look out for:

- the ひらがな symbols after each 漢字 serve to show the tense of the verb.
- ます endings indicate the present or future (for instance, **I eat/ will eat**).
- ました indicates the past (e.g. **I ate**).
- the *kunyomi* (Japanese reading) is used for single 漢字 verbs with ひらがな endings.
- unfamiliar readings are indicated in ふりがな (*furigana*) which is ひらがな written above 漢字 to show the pronunciation. (In some texts it may be written below or beside 漢字.)

Now see if you can read these verbs:

a た
食べます (I eat)   た
食べました (I ate)

b の
飲みます (I drink)   の
飲みました (I drank)

c み
見ます (I look)   み
見ました (I looked)

d か
書きます (I write)   か
書きました (I wrote)

e はな
話します (I talk)   はな
話しました (I talked)

練習十 *Activity 10*

In Unit 4, you worked out the meanings of a set of Japanese sentences by identifying the key 漢字 words. The same sentences now follow again, but this time you are going to practise reading the whole sentence in Japanese. You can do this now because you have learned to read ひらがな. The readings for the 漢字 words or parts of words are given in ふりがな (*furigana*). Check the English meanings of the sentences by referring back to Unit 4. Read out loud!

は、を、に and が have grammar functions which you will learn more about in Unit 10. When は has this function, it is pronounced wa (whereas when it is used as part of a word, it is pronounced in the usual way as ha).

1 女 の人 は 日本語 を 学 びました。
　おんな　　ひと　　　にほんご　　　まな

2 女 の子 は 土曜日 に 休 みました。
　おんな　こ　　　どようび　　やす

3 男 の人 は 月を 見 ました。
　おとこ　ひと　　つき　　み

4 林 さん は 森田 さんに 話 しました。
　はやし　　もりた　　はな

5 男 の子 は 馬 が 好きです。
　おとこ　こ　　うま　　す

6 女 の人 は 竹 の 子を 食べました。
　おんな　ひと　　たけ　こ　た

7 山田 さんは 車 を売 りました。
　やまだ　　くるま　う

5.10 終りに Conclusion

In this unit, you have learned the 46 basic ひらがな symbols plus related sounds and rules. You have had the chance to write them and to read words and phrases in ひらがな. You have learned the two main uses of ひらがな:

- to write words not normally written in 漢字
- to indicate grammar functions and word endings.

You will come across ひらがな again in Unit 10 and you can refer back to this unit whenever you need to, so do not worry if you have not taken everything in with the first attempt!

5.11 Five things to remember

Five important things to remember from Unit 5:

- Every *hiragana* symbol represents a sound (phoneme).
- All Japanese text could be written in *hiragana*, but *kanji* provide visual clues, break up the text making it easier to scan and make texts more sophisticated.
- There are 46 basic *hiragana* symbols, but 104 if you include contracted sounds and sounds with *tenten/maru*.
- There is a correct order in which to write *hiragana* symbols. Remember these two basic rules: horizontal strokes are written left to right; vertical/diagonal strokes from top to bottom.
- A small つ (*tsu*) is not spoken – it is an indication to pause slightly before saying the next sound – がんばって (gamba - *pause* - te – **good luck!**).

6

....

第六課
Unit 6

In this unit, you will:

- *learn to decode the meanings of 39 new 漢字*
- *learn to read more compound 漢字 words*
- *try some activities to review all the 漢字 you have learned so far*
- *learn to read and write 11 adjectives (describing words)*

6.1 はじめに Introduction

In Units 1 and 2, you looked at 漢字 which derive from pictures of nature. Here is a selection of them. Can you remember their meanings?

a 土		**b** 木		**c** 女		**d** 石	
e 口		**f** 馬		**g** 日		**h** 月	

6.2 Work it out!

As you did in Units 1 and 2, see if you can match the following pictures (1–10) with the correct 漢字 (a–j).

1 tall/high

2 old

3 big

4 small

5 bird

6 rice

7 thread

8 cow

9 axe

10 stand

a 立 **b** 高 **c** 鳥 **d** 米 **e** 大
f 斤 **g** 牛 **h** 古 **i** 糸 **j** 小

How did you get on? Check your answers at the back, then look at the development sequence from picture to modern *kanji* that follows.

1 高
tall/high

2 古
old

3 大
big

4 小
small

5 鳥
bird

6 米
rice

7 糸
thread

8 牛
cow

9 斤
axe

10 立
stand

練習一 *Activity 1*

Match the 漢字 in the left column (a–j) with the English meanings in the right column (1–10). Look back at the 漢字 pictures if you need to remind yourself of the meanings.

a 牛

b 斤

c 高

1 small

2 big

3 old

d	立	**4**	tall/high (also means expensive)
e	糸	**5**	bird
f	古	**6**	cow
g	小	**7**	rice
h	鳥	**8**	thread
i	大	**9**	axe
j	米	**10**	stand (up)

6.3 Decoding kanji

About 2–3% of 漢字 derive from simple pictorial representations. As you have already learned, many of these simple pictorial 漢字 are also used as components in more complex 漢字. You will be looking at this in more detail in Unit 7, but one of the purposes of this unit is to introduce you to some more simple 漢字 which will help you in this unit, and later, to decode the meaning and make-up of other more complex 漢字.

Let us start with four new 漢字 and look at how their components can be brought together into a story to give the meaning.

1 母   (**mother**). You can see the outline of 女 (**woman**) in this

漢字 → 母 The two short strokes within the 漢字

indicate breasts, hence **mother**.

2 安   (**cheap, safe**). Again, you can see the 漢字 for **woman**. The component above is like a hat or covering. So the 漢字 looks like a **woman** wearing a **cheap hat!**

3 広   (**wide, spacious**). The left side of this 漢字 should remind you of a cliff or cave.
Within it is a triangular shape with a **wide** base (it also looks like a **wide** nose!).

4 新 (new). You have learned two of these components in this unit. The top left is 立 (stand (up)), the right side is 斤 (axe). The remaining component (bottom left) is 木 (tree).

Story: Cut down a **standing tree** and get **new** wood.

練習二 Activity 2

Now you are going to try to link new 漢字 with stories to establish their meanings. Three of the following 漢字 represent colours (**blue, white, black**) and the other two mean **father** and **rain**. Which is which? Look at the 漢字, read the stories and link them up.

a 黑   **b** 白   **c** 青   **d** 父   **e** 雨

1 **Rain.** This 漢字 looks like drops of **rain** against a window.
2 **White.** The components, **sun** (日) and **ray** (short stroke) depict the **white** rays of the sun.
3 **Father.** He has a long moustache and dimples in his cheeks!
4 **Black.** The components – **rice field**, **earth** and **fire** (four short 'flamelike' strokes) – depict the deep black colour which the earth turns when the rice stubble is burned after the harvest.
5 **Blue.** This 漢字 also means **green** (for example, the colour of traffic lights and apples). Its components are **earth** with an extra horizontal line, which means plants growing out of the ground, and **moon**. Young plants are green, and we speak of a **blue** moon.

練習三 Activity 3

As in Activity 1, you are going to see how well you can remember the 漢字 you have been introduced to in this section (nine in total). Link the 漢字 (a–i) to the English meaning (1–9).

a 安	**1** father	f 母	**6** cheap, safe
b 雨	**2** mother	g 白	**7** wide, spacious
c 青	**3** white	h 黒	**8** new
d 新	**4** black	i 父	**9** rain
e 広	**5** blue, green		

6.4 Abstract kanji

In Unit 3, you learned the 漢字 for numbers (一、二、三、 etc.). These are from a small group of 漢字 which depict abstract ideas using shapes and lines. The 漢字 for the words **above, below** and **inside** are formed in a similar way. Look at these 漢字:

1 上 (**above, on top**) has a baseline with a 't' shape **above** it.

2 下 (**below, under**) has a baseline with a 't' shape **below** it.

3 中 (**inside, middle**) is a box with a line through the **middle**.

Insight

You can also imagine 上 and 下 to look like the top and roots of a plant.

You have now learned 22 new 漢字 in this unit. Let us review them, grouping them together by theme.

Colours

青 (*blue*)　　白 (*white*)　　黒 (*black*)

Adjectives (describing words)

大 (*big*)   小 (*small*)   古 (*old*)   新 (*new*)
高 (*tall, expensive*)   安 (*cheap, safe*)   広 (*wide*)

People, animals

母 (*mother*)   父 (*father*)   牛 (*cow*)   鳥 (*bird*)

Nature, basic items

雨 (*rain*)   米 (*rice*)   斤 (*axe*)   糸 (*thread*)

Position

上 (*above*)   下 (*below*)   中 (*inside*)   立 (*stand up*)

6.5 Complex kanji

In Units 2 and 4, you learned that more complex 漢字 are made from combinations of simpler 漢字. These simpler 漢字 become components of the more complex ones. Examples you have learned include 男 (*man*), 好 (*like*) and 聞 (*listen*). Now let us look at 漢字 you have learned in this unit which are also used as components in more complex 漢字.

雨 **Rain** is used as a component of more complex 漢字 to indicate types of weather (with rain as their basis), such as:

雲 **Cloud**. The lower components are *two* and *triangle shape* – think of them as 'two cloud shapes'!

曇 **Cloudy weather**. The lower part is cloud, and the upper component is 日 (*sun*). Cloudy weather blocks out the sun!

雪 **Snow** ('frozen rain'). The lower component (ヨ) looks like 山 (*mountain*) on its side. Think of snow-covered mountains!

雷 **Thunder.** The lower component is rice field, a place where farmers would be very aware of thunderstorms.

電 **Electric** is an interesting progression from *thunder*. This time, you can see a flash of lightning through the rice field – and lightning creates electricity!

練習四 *Activity 4*

You are going to try identifying more complex 漢字 by looking at the components (a–h) and linking them into a meaning (1–8). Here are the 漢字:

a 犬   **b** 島   **c** 音   **d** 辛

e 少   **f** 鳩   **g** 霜   **h** 尖

Story meanings

1 *Meaning*: **island.** Japan is made up of many, many small islands, often just rocky hills in the sea with only birds living on them. This 漢字, therefore, is a depiction of a **bird** sitting (you can't see its tail feathers) on a **mountain**.
2 *Meaning*: **dove, pigeon.** The components **bird** and **nine** represent a dove.
3 *Meaning*: **hot/bitter** (taste). The components **stand up** and **ten** combine to give an image of strong flavours which make the taste buds stand up to the power of ten!
4 *Meaning*: **dog.** The components **big** + short stroke depict a large dog with its tongue hanging out!
5 *Meaning*: **sound, noise.** Components: **stand up** and **sun.** Stand in the sun and listen to the sounds.
6 *Meaning*: **pointed, tapered.** Components **big** and **small.** Put simply, tapering to a point involves something becoming smaller.
7 *Meaning*: **few, a little.** Components: **small** and a diagonal stroke.
8 *Meaning*: **frost.** Components: **rain, tree** and **eye.** Frost (made from rain) on trees looks like millions of sparkling eyes.

Finally, the 漢字 for **fat** is 太. This looks very similar to 犬 (**dog**). You can distinguish them by thinking of the short stroke in **dog** as the tongue and of the short stroke in **fat** as a marker indicating the widest or fattest part of the 漢字.

In this section of *kanji* build-up, you have been introduced to 14 new 漢字. They are listed here. Can you remember their meanings? Check back through the section if there are any you are unsure about.

雪、雲、電、雷、霜、曇、犬、太、少、辛、
音、尖、鳩、島。

6.6 Kanji compounds 1

Remember that kanji compounds are words created from two or more 漢字. You have come across examples of these in Units 1–4. Words such as 人口 (**population**), 日曜日 (**Sunday**) and 食物 (**food**) are some of the 漢字 compounds you have learned so far.

The next two activities are designed to get you thinking about the meanings of some new 漢字 compound words using the 漢字 you have been introduced to in this unit plus others you have learned in earlier units.

練習五 *Activity 5*

This activity uses combinations of 漢字 you have learned in this unit only. Match the kanji compounds in the box with the English meanings from the list beneath it.

a 白鳥	**b** 大雨	**c** 父母	**d** 青白
e 小犬	**f** 小牛	**g** 広大	**h** 白米

Meanings

1 vast **2** swan **3** calf **4** puppy, small dog **5** parents
6 polished (white) rice **7** pale; blue-white **8** heavy rain

練習六 *Activity 6*

This activity combines 漢字 from this unit with some you have
learned from previous units. Those from previous units are:

年 (year)、 学 (study)、 女 (woman)、 車 (vehicle)、
手 (hand)、 人 (person)、 口 (mouth)、 目 (eye)、
聞 (listen)、 話 (talk)、 中 (middle)

Again, match each 漢字 word from the box (a–q) with its English
meaning (1–17). The bracketed information gives the literal meaning
in cases where the meaning may not be immediately obvious.

```
a 新年    b 青年    c 少年    d 少女    e 大学
f 小人    g 大人    h 糸口    i 年上    j 目上
k 上手    l 下手    m 新車    n 新聞    o 電車
p 電話    q 中古車
```

1 university (*big study*)
2 train (*electric vehicle*)
3 good at (*upper hand*)
4 bad at (*lower hand*)
5 youth (*blue years* = *innocence*)
6 your superiors (their *eye level* is *above you*)
7 child (*small person*)
8 adult (*big person*)
9 clue (*the thread mouth*!)
10 telephone (*electric talk*)
11 new year
12 older [than you] (*years above*)
13 boy (*few years*)
14 girl (*a few / a little bit a woman*)
15 new car
16 second-hand car (*in the middle of being old*)
17 newspaper (*newly heard*)

Check your answers before moving on to the next section.

6.7 Kanji compounds 2

Finally in this section, you are going to extend your knowledge of 漢字 compounds a little further by learning three new 漢字 and looking at how these are used in combination with 漢字 you have learned in this unit to make new words.

1 国   means **country** and is the depiction of a king (玉… lit. **jewel**) within the boundaries (囗) of his kingdom. Examples of its usage are:

米国	**rice country** is the Japanese word for **America**. (The rice grown in America is short-grained like Japanese rice and often packaged and sold as Japanese rice.)
中米	**middle rice** is the Japanese word for **Central America**.
中国	**middle country** means **China** (the central country of Asia).
母国	**mother country** means exactly that, the country you originate from.
島国	**island country** (such as Japan, Britain and Australia).

2 肉   means **meat** or **flesh**. You can see two people (人) hanging from a frame!

牛肉	**cow meat** means **beef**.
鳥肉	**bird meat** means **chicken**.

3 校   means **school**. The left side, **tree** (木) indicates a wooden building (Japanese schools were traditionally made of wood) and the right side is **father** (父) wearing a hat. Think of this as a teacher.

学校	**study school** means **school**.
小学校	**small school** means **elementary** or **primary school**.
中学校	means **middle school** or **junior high school**.

高校　　means **high school** (abbreviated version of
高等学校).

練習七 *Activity 7*

In this unit, you have been introduced to 36 new 漢字
compounds. You can see them all in the following list; your task is
to test your memory by writing the meanings in the brackets after
each word. Then check your answers by looking back through
Sections 6.6 and 6.7.

白鳥	( )	大雨	( )
小犬	( )	小牛	( )
新年	( )	青年	( )
大学	( )	小人	( )
年上	( )	目上	( )
新車	( )	新聞	( )
中国	( )	母国	( )
鳥肉	( )	学校	( )
高校	( )	電車	( )
父母	( )	青白	( )
広大	( )	白米	( )
少年	( )	少女	( )
大人	( )	糸口	( )
上手	( )	下手	( )
米国	( )	中米	( )
島国	( )	牛肉	( )
小学校	( )	中学校	( )
電話	( )	中古車	( )

6.8 漢字の読み方 How to read kanji

In this section, you are going to learn to say the 11 adjectives (describing words) learned in this unit, in Japanese. Look up the *kunyomi* (**Japanese reading**) for the following 漢字 in the unit chart at the back of the book.

高、安、小、大、少*、古、新、太、広、白

*少 has two *kunyomi* – *sukuna(i)* means **few**; *suko(shi)* means **a little**.

Insight

Notice that part of the reading is written in brackets. This is the part which is written in ひらがな. For example: taka(i) is written 高い meaning tall, expensive.

Memorize the whole reading, including the part in brackets, then try the activity that follows.

練習八 *Activity 8*

You are now going to practise reading the 11 adjectives as complete words, including the ひらがな endings. Even if you have not yet worked through Unit 5, you can still do this, because the whole word is given in the unit chart and the answers are given at the back of the book.

a 高い   **b** 安い   **c** 小さい   **d** 大きい
e 少い   **f** 少し   **g** 古い   **h** 新しい
i 太い   **j** 広い   **k** 白い

6.9 書く練習五 Writing practice 5

In Units 1 and 2, you learned some general rules for writing 漢字. You put these into practice in Unit 3 to write 漢字 numbers and in Unit 4 to write 漢字 verbs. Now you are going to learn to write the ten 漢字 from Activity 8. (Remember that the kanji 少 represents two meanings – **few** and **a little**.)

Insight

Use squared paper and focus on the proportions and overall balance of each 漢字. Once you feel confident, see if you can write them from memory. Keep saying the meaning (and the readings) to yourself as you write them to help fix all the different elements into your memory. In the case of the adjectives old and new, part of each kanji is already known to you (mouth and tree), so the stroke order is not given for these parts. You can look up the stroke order for mouth and tree in Section 1.6 (Writing practice 1).

大	大	一	ナ	大
小	小	丨	小	小
少	少	丨	小	小	少
古	古	一	十	古
新	新
丶	亠	十	立	立
亲	新	新	新	新
太	太	一	ナ	大	太
広	広
丶	亠	广	広	広

6.10 終りに Conclusion

In this unit, you have been introduced to a total of 39 single 漢字 through picture association and through analysing their component parts. You have also learned 36 new 漢字 compounds and have practised reading and writing the 漢字 words for 11 adjectives. Units 1–6 have altogether introduced you to 97 single 漢字, 100 漢字 compounds (including 13 surnames) and the whole ひらがな syllabary! おめでとう (*omedetō*) Congratulations!

Insight

Of course, you might not remember all or even most of these new kanji and hiragana, but the purpose of this book is to help you understand more about Japanese script, about how it is made up and to find ways for you to break the 漢字 code and to build on your learning. Even Japanese people forget 漢字 from time to time; it takes time and practice to build up your knowledge of them. But remember – Japanese script can be fun to learn, too!

6.11 テスト Test yourself

a The test at the end of Unit 4 contained a summary of all the single 漢字 you had learned up to that point. This activity pulls together all the single 漢字 you have learned in this unit. Can you identify them all? They are in ascending order of stroke number. The answers are at the back, but do not worry if you cannot do them all on the first attempt – you can keep coming back to this activity!

1 上	2 下	3 小	4 大	5 中	6 犬
7 太	8 少	9 斤	10 父	11 牛	12 立
13 古	14 母	15 広	16 白	17 米	18 安
19 糸	20 尖	21 肉	22 辛	23 雨	24 青
25 国	26 音	27 高	28 島	29 校	30 黒
31 鳥	32 雪	33 雲	34 新	35 雷	36 電
37 鳩	38 曇	39 霜			

b This activity is designed to test how well you remember the compound words you have learned so far. The surnames are not included; you can review these by turning to Activity 7 of Unit 2. The words below are grouped by theme (loosely in some cases!). What do they mean in English?

Days of the week

1 日曜日　　　2 土曜日　　　3 水曜日
4 火曜日

School and study

5 入学　　　　6 小学校　　　7 中学校
8 高校　　　　9 休学　　　　10 見学

Countries

11 日本　　12 中国　　13 米国
14 中米　　15 母国　　16 島国

Food and drink

17 牛肉　　18 鳥肉　　19 食物
20 飲物　　21 白米　　22 飲水

Transport

23 電車　　24 新車　　25 中古車
26 馬車　　27 人力車

Animals

28 小犬　　29 小牛　　30 白鳥

People

31 父母　　32 小人　　33 大人
34 少年　　35 少女　　36 女子

Shopping and travel

37 買物　　38 見物　　39 入口
40 出口　　41 休日

7

第七課
Unit 7

In this unit, you will:
- *learn about the different types of* 漢字
- *learn more about* 漢字 *radicals and components*
- *identify* 漢字 *meanings from their radical*
- *learn to write* 漢字 *in the correct proportions*

7.1 はじめに Introduction

In Units 2, 4 and 6, you looked at how simpler 漢字 are used as components of more complex ones. Look back over these units if you find now or later that you need to refresh your memory. In this unit, you are going to look in more depth at ways you can crack the code for more complex 漢字. First of all, you are going to test your memory of some of the complex 漢字 you have learned so far.

1 What are the meanings of the 漢字 that follow?

a 林	b 森	c 男	d 好	e 明	f 聞
g 見	h 書	i 言	j 売	k 読	l 話
m 買	n 休	o 出	p 学		

2 What are the meanings of the left sides of the 漢字 in this list? (You will not know the whole meaning at this stage.) Refer to Section 4.2 if you need more information about the left side of **a**.

a 体 **b** 唱 **c** 埋 **d** 妹 **e** 孫 **f** 時
g 肘 **h** 村 **i** 畑 **j** 町 **k** 眠 **l** 談
m 針 **n** 転

7.2 Types of kanji

There are a number of ways in which 漢字 have been developed. You are already familiar with the first three of these categories:

1 Pictorial kanji

These fairly simple 漢字 derive from pictures of nature. Examples are 山 (**mountain**), 川 (**river**) and 人 (**person**). They make up about 2–3% of all 漢字.

2 Simple abstract kanji

These 漢字 convey abstract ideas through symbols, for example, the numbers (Unit 3). There are only a very few of this kind.

3 Complex pictorial kanji

These are made up of two or more basic pictorial 漢字 which together convey a new meaning. Examples are 林 (**wood**), 男 (**man**) and 明 (**bright**), but the second activity in the introduction to this unit has more examples which you will be learning. Again, this type of 漢字 makes up about 2–3% of all 漢字.

Part of the 漢字 conveys the general meaning and part conveys the pronunciation (*onyomi* or Chinese reading). By identifying the component parts, you have a clue to the meaning and how to say it. Examples (from the second activity in the Introduction above) include 時 (**time**) and 転 (**turn**). About 90% of 漢字 belong to this group.

This unit is going to focus on categories 3 and 4, and you are going to learn ways of cracking the 漢字 code!

7.3 Kanji components

As you have already learned, more complex 漢字 are made up of simpler ones which we have called **components**. One of these components, known as the **radical**, often gives a clue to the general meaning of the whole 漢字. Many radicals are themselves 漢字, usually of the simple pictorial kind. In dictionaries, 漢字 are grouped by their radical (same radical, same group). You will learn more about this later in the unit.

According to the traditional Chinese classification, there are 214 radicals in total. The purpose of this unit is to introduce you to a few of the more common radicals and to make you familiar with the idea of radicals so that you have a solid foundation to build on.

Insight

In the second activity in the introduction, you identified the left part of each 漢字. You were, in fact, identifying the radical in this activity – the most common location of a radical is on the left side of a 漢字.

練習一 Activity 1

In this activity, you will have a go at identifying new 漢字 (a–l) which are formed by combining two or more pictorial 漢字

(category 3 of explanation). You have already come across some of these new 漢字 in the second activity in the introduction to this unit. Beneath a–l are a number of stories and meanings.
See if you can match each 漢字 with a story and meaning by looking at the components that make up the 漢字.

a 信 **b** 唱 **c** 畑 **d** 談 **e** 孫 **f** 鳴
g 語 **h** 炎 **i** 焚 **j** 埋 **k** 旦 **l** 姦

Stories and meanings

1 **Three women** together are very wicked! *Meaning*: **wickedness**
2 Heaping **fire** upon **fire** creates a blaze. *Meaning*: **blaze, flame**
3 A **fire** burning **wood** (**two trees**). *Meaning*: **burn, kindle**
4 A **field** burnt by **fire** is ready for cultivation. *Meaning*: **cultivated field**
5 The **mouth** of the **bird** creates birdsong. *Meaning*: **cry, chirp** (of birds, animals)
6 A **person's words** are to be believed. *Meaning*: **believe**
7 The **three mouths** (the **lines in two** look like tongues) chanted in unison. *Meaning*: **chant, recite**
8 They dug up the **rice field** and buried the treasure in the **earth** **beneath**. *Meaning*: **be buried**
9 The visual image is 'speaking fiery words'. *Meaning*: **discussion, conversation**
10 'Speaking five mouths'. In other words, five languages. *Meaning*: **language(s)**
11 The **sun** rising above the **horizon**. *Meaning*: **dawn**
12 The **child** is attached to its ancestors by a genetic **thread** (there is a short line above the thread which is attached to the child). *Meaning*: **grandchild**

7.4 More about radicals and components

In the last activity, you arrived at the meaning of the 漢字 by linking the components into a story. You can do this with many

漢字; even though sometimes the story or link may seem far-fetched, if the meanings of the components are kept consistent, this method can be a very useful code-breaker and memory 'jog' when learning new 漢字.

You have already learned in this unit that the radical of a 漢字 usually conveys its general meaning. Let us look at this in more detail using the radical 言 (**say**). Some 漢字 follow which contain this radical (on the left side):

記 (**narrative, history**)	訳 (**translation**)
証 (**proof, certificate**)	調 (**tune**)
談 (**conversation**)	詩 (**poem**)
語 (**language**)	課 (**lesson**)

These examples show that the radical indicates a general link with the meaning of speech or words (including musical 'words' or notes in the case of 調 – tune). Now let us look at some of the more common radicals.

Insight

Remember that there are 214 radicals altogether, but the aim of this unit is to introduce you to the idea of radicals and to show you ways in which they can be helpful in learning 漢字.

Here are the left-hand radicals which you identified in the second activity in the introduction. You learned the meanings in earlier units.

人 (person)	口 (mouth)	土 (earth)
女 (woman)	日 (sun, day)	子 (child)
月 (moon)	木 (tree)	火 (fire)
田 (rice field)	目 (eye)	言 (say; words)
金 (gold, metal) (as a radical, it normally means metal)		
車 (car, vehicle, wheel)		

You have already learned that a 漢字 may change shape slightly when used as a radical. Here are some examples (the radical is on the left).

1 Radicals may appear 'squashed' 埋 (radical = **earth**)

2 Radicals may have some shorter strokes 林 (radical = **tree**)

3 Radicals may change their shape 体 (radical = **person**)

Here are two more useful radicals whose shape differs from the 漢字 you have met already:

水 (**water**) as a left-hand radical → 泊 (looks like three splashes of water)

手 (**hand**) as a left-hand radical → 折 (squashed and the top line has gone)

Insight

One more point to note before you begin the next activity is that two of the radicals already mentioned have two meanings. They are:

月 (moon); this has the second meaning flesh (from a 'squashed' version of 肉 – flesh/meat)

日 (sun); this can also take the meaning speak (from 曰 (to speak) – 'a tongue in a mouth' – although this is rare)

練習二 *Activity 2*

In this activity, you will look at a number of 漢字 with the radical missing. The meaning of the full 漢字 is given (plus a story where appropriate) and you have to decide which radical (from those listed opposite) will complete the 漢字 (the answers are at the end of the activity). Here is an example to help you:

舌 *Components*: **tongue** and **mouth**. *Story*: You must drink water to live. *Meaning*: **to live**

Answer: 活 (radical = *water*).

a 本　*Components*: **root** (of tree). *Story*: The root/origin of a person is their body. *Meaning*: **body**

b 丁　*Component*: a **marker** or **post**. *Story*: Rice fields mark a town's boundaries. *Meaning*: **town**

c 寸　*Component*: **measurement**. *Story*: The villagers measured and cut wood to make their homes. *Meaning*: **village**

d 未　*Components*: **tree** and **short top branches** = not yet (that is, not yet a fully grown tree) *Story*: someone who is not yet a woman. *Meaning*: **younger sister**

e 丁　*Component*: a **marker** or **post**. *Story*: Fire on a post makes a lamp to mark your way. *Meaning*: **lamp**

f 斤　*Component*: **axe**. *Story*: With his hand, he wielded the axe to break the object. *Meaning*: **to break, snap, fold**

g 民　*Component*: **people, nation**. *Story*: The people closed their eyes and slept. *Meaning*: **sleep**

h 犬　*Component*: **dog**. *Story*: Dogs bark with their mouths. *Meaning*: **to bark**

i 寸　*Component*: **measurement**. *Story*: part of the body (flesh) used as an old measurement, from elbow to fingertip. *Meaning*: **elbow**

j 白　*Component*: **white**. *Story*: The hotel we stayed at had water and clean, white towels. *Meaning*: **to stay at**

k 十　*Component*: **ten**, but imagine it to be a needle with thread coming out of it (horizontal line). *Story*: Needles are made of metal. *Meaning*: **needle**

l 二 + 厶　*Components*: **two** (+ a shape which looks like a nose! In the 漢字 the two is above the nose). *Story*: The car's two wheels rotate. *Meaning*: **to rotate, turn**

m 寺　*Components*: **earth** and **measurement** = temple (Think of Buddhist priests plotting out the area of land before building the temple.) *Story*: The temple bell struck each hour all through the day. Meaning: **time, hour**

How did you get on? Here are the 漢字 you have identified, complete with their radical and full meaning. Think about how the radical gives a clue to the general meaning and how you can fit the components together into a story.

a 体 (body)　　　　**b** 町 (town)　　　**c** 村 (village)

d 妹 (younger sister)　**e** 灯 (lamp)　　**f** 折 (fold, snap)

g 眠 (sleep)　　　　**h** 吠 (bark)　　　**i** 肘 (elbow)

j 泊 (stay at)　　　　**k** 針 (needle)　　**l** 転 (turn)

m 時 (time)

練習三 *Activity 3*

In the second activity in the introduction to this unit, you identified the left-hand radicals of 漢字, but not the full meaning. You have now come across all these meanings, so turn back to that activity in Section 7.1, and see if you can identify all the 漢字. The answers are in Activities 1 and 2.

7.5 Locating the radical

So far, you have identified radicals on the left side of 漢字. This is the most common position of a radical, but not the only one. Here are the other locations with examples (the radical is in brackets).

right side	形 *shape* (彡)	都 *capital* (阝)
above	茶 *tea* (艹)	安 *cheap* (宀)
below	楽 *enjoyable* (木)	急 *emergency* (心)
surround – complete	国 *country* (囗)	
surround – partial	店 *shop* (广)	道 *road, way* (辶)
	聞 *listen* (門)	

Some radicals are located in more than one position. For example, 木 (**tree**) is found:

1 left side (林 woods)

2 above (査 investigate)

3 below (楽 enjoy)

And in different positions, some radicals change their shape. For example, 火 (fire):

1 left side 畑 (field)

2 below 煮 (boil) Here it looks like four small flames.

And 心 (heart):

1 left side 情 (feeling)

2 below 急 (emergency)

練習四 *Activity 4*

The box that follows contains some common radicals found in the **right-hand**, **above**, **below** or **surround** positions. Their names/meanings are given in brackets.

艹 (*vegetation*)	欠 (*yawn*)	气 (*vapour*)
阝 (*village*)	亠 (*lid*)	宀 (*hat!*)
竹 (*bamboo*)	冖 (*cover*)	火 or 灬 (*fire*)
雨 (*rain*)	囗 (*enclosure*)	穴 (*hole*)
		忄 or 心 (*heart*)

Look at the 漢字 a–m that follow and decide: 1 which is its radical (from the box above) and 2 where its radical is located.

Here is an example to help you. Think as well how the radical may indicate the general meaning.

例 *Rei* 芋 (*potato*) **1** vegetation radical
2 above (link: a potato is a vegetable)

---

a 安 (*cheap*) **b** 花 (*flower*)
c 京 (*capital city*) **d** 都 (*large city*)
e 図 (*picture, diagram*) **f** 歌 (*song*)
g 筆 (*writing brush*) **h** 黒 (*black*)
i 空 (*air, sky*) **j** 軍 (*army*)
k 気 (*spirit*) **l** 思 (*think*)
m 雪 (*snow*)

7.6 漢字の読み方 How to read kanji

It has already been mentioned earlier on in this unit that as well as the radical often giving the general meaning of 漢字, the other component(s) sometimes indicate the reading (onyomi). Below are six 漢字 whose right sides (or, in the case of **temple**, the whole 漢字) are all the same and are read either JI or SHI.

寺 (**temple**) *JI*   時 (**time**) *JI*   持 (**hold**) *JI*
侍 (**samurai**) *JI*   崎 (**tower, soar**) *JI*   詩 (**poem**) *SHI*

Notice how the left side (the radical) gives a clue to the meaning. We have discussed some already, for example, 詩 (**poem**) has the radical 言 (**say, words**). 持 (**hold**) has the radical 手 (**hand** – remember it changes its shape slightly). Look at the radicals of the others and think about how these give a pointer to their meaning. (The radical for temple is **earth**.)

練習五 *Activity 5*

This activity gets you to look at 漢字 whose right sides and onyomi reading are the same. You will first be given the right side (this can stand alone as a 漢字 too) and then will choose from a selection of radicals (the full 漢字 is also given in brackets) which one gives the full 漢字 its particular meaning. Refer to Sections 7.4 and 7.5 if you cannot remember the meaning of a radical. The first one has the answers immediately after, to help you get started.

Right side: 召 (SHŌ) **Meaning:** call, send for, summon

Radicals (漢字)	Meanings	
a 手 (招)	**i** beckon, invite	( )
b 日 (昭)	**ii** inherit	( )
c 水 (沼)	**iii** imperial edict, decree	( )
d 糸 (紹)	**iv** clear, bright	( )
e 言 (詔)	**v** swamp, marsh	( )

Answers

i = **a** = 招 (link: beckon with your hand)

ii = **d** = 紹 (link: inheritance 'thread' to relatives)

iii = **e** = 詔 (link: spoken 'summons' = decree)

iv = **b** = 昭 (link: sun and bright)

v = **c** = 沼 (link: swamps are watery)

Insight

Before you try the rest of the activity, look at the example above.

- Sometimes the right-side meaning can be clearly included in the link (as in i–iii); sometimes it is not quite so clear (as in iv and v).

- The radicals are given in their full 漢字 form, but they may change shape when used as part of a 漢字 (as in i and v).

1 Right side: 青 (SEI) Meaning: blue

Radicals	（漢字）	Meanings	
a 心 (*heart*)	（情）	**i** purify, cleanse	( )
b 日	（晴）	**ii** request, ask	( )
c 水	（清）	**iii** spirit/white rice/purity	( )
d 言	（請）	**iv** fine weather, clear up	( )
e 米 (*rice*)	（精）	**v** feeling, emotion	( )

2 Right side: 乍 (SAKU) No meaning

Radicals	（漢字）	Meanings	
a 日	（昨）	**i** yesterday, previous	( )
b 人	（作）	**ii** make, create	( )
c 火	（炸）	**iii** vinegar	( )
d 酉 (*liquid, alcohol*)	（酢）	**iv** explosion	( )

3 Right side: 干 (KAN) Meaning: get dry, parch

Radicals	（漢字）	Meanings	
a 手	（扞）	**i** wickedness, mischief	( )
b 女	（奸）	**ii** liver	( )
c 水	（汗）	**iii** perspire	( )
d 月 (*flesh*)	（肝）	**iv** snore	( )
e 鼻 (*nose*)	（鼾）	**v** pole, rod	( )
f 竹	（竿）	**vi** restrain	( )
g 日	（旱）	**vii** drought, dry weather	( )

7.7 Using kanji dictionaries

How did you get on in the last activity? It is important to restate at this stage that although many 漢字 have a part which gives a clue to the reading (of the onyomi) and that the radical often gives a clue to the general meaning, they do not all fall into these categories. However, remember, you can really begin to make inroads into your learning of 漢字 when you have some rules and clues like this to help you.

Knowing about radicals does become essential when you start to use a 漢字 dictionary. As you learned in **Only got ten minutes?**, the Japanese Ministry of Education made a list of 1,942 漢字 which are essential to know in everyday communication. However, there are many more 漢字 than this, which are used in specialist, academic and pre-war writings and documents. (Compare this situation with the many more words in an English dictionary than most people know or use in everyday life.) A 漢字 dictionary, therefore, may have 5,000 or more entries, but many of these are not in common usage.

How kanji dictionaries work

1 Identify the radical

The most commonly used 漢字 dictionary for non-Japanese people is the *Japanese–English Character Dictionary* by Andrew Nelson (but often referred to simply as 'Nelson'). 漢字 are traditionally looked up in a dictionary by first identifying the radical and then locating the section where all 漢字 with this radical are grouped. Radicals are ordered by their number of strokes, from those of one stroke through to those of 16 or 17 (in Nelson). The number and type of radical does vary slightly from dictionary to dictionary. In Nelson, each radical is numbered (from 1 to 214), and its number is clearly printed at the top of every page so that it is easy to turn to the section you are looking for. There is a list of all the radicals with their number on the inside front cover.

2 Count the remaining strokes

Once you have identified the radical and turned to the relevant section, you next count the number of remaining strokes in the 漢字 you are looking up, excluding the radical stroke number. All 漢字 with the same radical are grouped according to the number of remaining strokes, from 1 through to the highest number (this can be up to 24 or more in the case of very complicated 漢字). As an extra guide, on the side of every page, the radical on that page is given in square brackets with the number of remaining strokes grouped on the same page printed next to it. For example,

 tells you that on this page are 漢字 with the radical 木 and four remaining strokes.

Summary of steps

Here are the steps for looking up a 漢字 (using Nelson). You want to find the meaning of 枝:

1 You identify the radical (木).
2 Count the number of its strokes (four).
3 Turn to the radical list on the inside cover, find 木 in the four-stroke group and make a note of its number (75).
4 Turn to section 75 (radical numbers are labelled at the top of each page).
5 Count the number of remaining strokes in 枝 (four).

6 Find the sub-section containing all 漢字 with four remaining strokes (quick reference at the side of each page).
7 Run your eye down the 漢字 listed until you find 枝.
   Meaning: branch

Identifying kanji by reading

If you know the pronunciation of the 漢字, you can look it up in the index at the back. Look through all 漢字 of the same reading until you see the one you want. There is a number next to it (every 漢字 is given its own number). Find this number by looking at the bottom edge of each page.

If at first you don't succeed ...

These steps are to help you get started if you want to use a 漢字 dictionary. Identifying the radical is not always easy (Nelson lists a series of steps at the beginning of the dictionary to assist you), and at the beginning you are bound to make mistakes in counting the number of strokes. But practice makes perfect (!) and with time and experience, you will be able to master looking up even very complicated 漢字. You can now see one reason why writing 漢字 correctly is so important – so that you can count how many strokes there are!

> **Insight**
>
> If you have access to a 漢字 dictionary, start by looking up the 漢字 you have been introduced to in this unit because the radical has already been identified for you. Alternatively, you may have the opportunity to use an electronic dictionary. These pocket-sized dictionaries normally hold (as a minimum) a Japanese–English dictionary, an English–Japanese dictionary, a Japanese–Japanese dictionary and a kanji dictionary. To access the kanji dictionary, however, you will essentially still need to follow the Nelson method – input radical and remaining strokes and/or reading – and you will need to practise and learn by your mistakes. However, they are handy gadgets if you wish to take your Japanese study further.

7.8 書く練習六 Writing practice 6

This is the last formal teaching section for writing in this book (although in Unit 10 you will be taught techniques for letter writing). This writing section is going to focus on the balance between the components of 漢字 (this has already been mentioned in Units 4 and 6). The 漢字 that follow have left sides which you are already familiar with as separate 漢字 but which change their shape slightly when used as radicals.

Insight

Copy the models carefully and notice changes in size, proportion and orientation of the radical. Look carefully at the way the whole 漢字 is written and do not let the different components divide and look like separate 漢字. As a rule of thumb, where there is a left and right side, the left side takes up one-third and the right side two-thirds.

The 漢字 you are going to learn to write are: 時 (**time**), 畑 (**cultivated field**), 村 (**village**), 泊 (**stay**), 針 (**needle**), 転 (turn), 妹 (**younger sister**), 埋 (**bury**) and 気 (**spirit**).

畑	畑			
丶	丷	少	火	灯
灯	炉	畑	畑	
村	村			
一	十	才	木	朳
村	村			
泊	泊			
丶	氵	氵	氵	
氵	泊	泊	泊	

針	針			
ノ	ᐟ	𠂉	𠂤	全
全	金	金	金一	針

転	転				
一	匸	厅	盲	百	亘
車	車一	車二	転	転	

妹	妹			
く	女	女	女一	
女二	奸	妹	妹	

7.9 終りに Conclusion

In this unit, you have covered more than 70 漢字 and 38 of the 214 radicals. However, the purpose of this unit was to introduce you to a technique of breaking down 漢字 into their component parts in order to extract meaning. Therefore, you are not expected to remember all the 漢字 which you have analysed during this unit. More important is the method you have been introduced to for decoding 漢字. The unit chart at the back, therefore, will not include all the 漢字 from this unit, but those learned in Activities 1 and 2 will be included for reference purposes.

Units 8, 9 and 10 will build on the knowledge and techniques that you have acquired from the first seven units of this book. Unit 8 covers general signs and information notices that you would see if you went to Japan; Unit 9 teaches カタカナ (*katakana*), the script for non-Japanese words; and Unit 10 offers you the chance to read a variety of Japanese texts.

Insight

You could take these units in any order – Unit 8, for example, teaches a large number of signs, so you might wish to 'dip into' that unit and then move on and return to it at a later date. It is up to you – you take control of your learning and if you find that something is difficult, or you just want a change, then move on to another unit.

7.10 テスト Test yourself

Below is a table of common radicals you have learned about in this unit (these are also *kanji* in their own right). Can you match each radical to its English meaning (1–20) below? Write the number after the radical.

Row 1: 人 ( )　手 ( )　口 ( )　目 ( )
Row 2: 子 ( )　女 ( )　水 ( )　火 ( )
Row 3: 田 ( )　木 ( )　月 ( )　日 ( )
Row 4: 金 ( )　車 ( )　土 ( )　言 ( )
Row 5: 雨 ( )　汽 ( )　心 ( )　竹 ( )

1 rain	**6** vapour	**11** gold/metal	**16** person
2 hand	**7** eye	**12** car/vehicle	**17** moon
3 mouth	**8** heart	**13** earth	**18** water
4 bamboo	**9** rice field	**14** say/words	**19** fire
5 sun	**10** child	**15** woman	**20** tree

8

第八課
Unit 8

In this unit, you will:

- *learn to read everyday signs and written information*
- *find clues and stories to help you remember new 漢字 words*
- *learn to recognize different writing styles*
- *decipher authentic everyday street signs and information*

8.1 About this unit

You will be introduced to a large number of 漢字 signs in this unit, with lots of clues to help you remember them. You are certainly not expected to remember them all, but to help you progress through this unit, the *kanji* build-up sections (Sections 8.6, 8.8 and 8.12) contain additional 漢字 words which you can leave out or come back to later if you find there is already enough new information to take in.

8.2 はじめに Introduction

When we travel around places, even within our own local area, we are constantly being informed by written signs and notices all around us. We pick out the information of use or interest (**sale, no entry, closed, danger**) and scan over the information we do not require. Visitors to Japan with no knowledge of written Japanese are struck almost immediately by the lack of information they are able to get from the signs and notices around them. There is some information in English, particularly in larger cities such as Tokyo, but your experience of Japan will be so much richer if you can understand some of the information that is written in Japanese.

When children first learn to read, they will obsessively read out all the shop names and road signs they see. In the same way, once you can recognize some of the common signs in Japanese, your eyes will feast on the new source of information open to you. Neon signs, advertisements, shop notices, tourist places, signs at stations – you find yourself able to operate much more efficiently and with more confidence because you can pick out the information you need and get to the places you want to go to.

This and the next unit will introduce you to some of the more common signs you may see around you in Japan. And not only in Japan – television programmes and films often show neon lights and other signs written in Japanese which, once you have completed this book, you can have a go at reading. And in Japanese department stores, restaurants and other speciality shops in large cities outside Japan, you see many signs and information written in Japanese. So there are plenty of opportunities to practise what you are going to learn in this unit.

8.3 Work it out!

First of all, you are going to try reading some common signs which you have already learned in previous units. The 漢字 words that follow have a box of English meanings beneath them (with clues and stories in brackets where necessary). Can you match them up?

a 入口	b 出口	c 女	d 男	e 上り
f 下り	g 電車	h 大人	i 小人	j お寺
k 学校	l 入国	m 出国	n 千円	o 休日

1 immigration (enter a country)	**8** holiday
2 train (electric vehicle)	**9** emigration (exit a country)
3 child (small person)	**10** adult (big person)
4 entrance	**11** school
5 up*	**12** exit
6 1,000 yen	**13** down*
7 men	**14** women
	15 temple

The answers in the back also have in brackets the number of the unit where the word was first introduced so that you can look it up again if you need to.

Insight

*A quick note about 上り (up) and 下り (down): these signs are used specifically on trains. 'Up' trains are travelling to Tokyo (from any direction) and 'down' trains are travelling away from Tokyo.

8.4 Kanji for places

There are a number of 漢字 which are used to indicate different types of places such as shops, rooms, public institutions and offices. Let us look at seven key ones. They are:

1 店 (*shop*) **2** 屋 (*store, roof*)

3 局 (*bureau, office*) **4** 所 (*place*)

5 場 (*place*) **6** 館 (*hall, large building*)

7 園 (*garden*)

Now let us look at each one in more detail.

1 店 (**shop**). The radical for this is 广, which means **dotted cliff** (厂 means **cliff**). Both these radicals indicate some type of enclosure. Think of it in this case as the roof and back wall of the shop. The front wall is, of course, a window and so is open. Inside the shop is 卜 (**fortune**) and 口 (**mouth**), together meaning 占 (**fortune telling**). To run a shop you have to be good at divining the customer's needs!

2 屋 (**store, roof**). The radical is 尸, meaning **flag**. Within it is 至 (**arrive**), which has within it 土 (**earth**). The flag is a banner advertising a newly built store (earth connection), waiting for the customers to arrive!

3 局 (**bureau, office**). The radical again is 尸 (**flag**) and within it is a mouth or opening enclosed on two sides. This 漢字 is used in words such as **post office**, so think of it as the glass counter behind which the office clerk sits. The **flag** is the board calling the next customer!

4 and **5** 所 and 場 (**place**). 所 is generally used to indicate an office or 'over-the-counter' type of place (tourist information office, foreign-exchange bureau), whereas 場 has the general meaning **grounds** (hence 土 – **earth** – as the radical). The radical for 所 is 戸 (**flag** with 'one' above it), and this by itself means **door**. You came across the right side in the previous unit, 斤 meaning **axe**. (Use the axe on the door to mark the spot or place!)

6 館 (**hall, large building**). This 漢字 is often used in public or government buildings. You should recognize the left side. It is the radical version of 食 (**food**). The right side 官 has the general meaning of **government**. Put together, large halls (such as concert halls, art galleries) are often funded by local government and you can usually buy refreshments, too!

7 園 (**garden**). This 漢字 is very easy to remember! First, there is the radical which you have already come across in the previous unit – 囗 which means **enclosure** or, in this case, the walls around a garden. Within the walls, there is 土 (**earth** – think of flower beds!), 口 (**mouth** – but think of this as a pond!) and off the 'pond' are a number of garden paths. Can you see it now?

練習一 *Activity 1*

Now let us put what you have learned so far into practice. Some 漢字 which you have already learned follow. The English meaning is in brackets. There are also some new 漢字 with some tips on how to remember them. Here are the 漢字:

売 (*sell*)	書 (*write*)	本 (*book*)	八百 (*800*)
肉 (*meat*)	飲 (*drink*)	車 (*vehicle*)	手 (*hand*)

> **Insight**
>
> Remember, if you want to review a 漢字 at any time, look up the English word in the index and it will refer you back to the page where you first learned it.

美術 **art** (the first 漢字 looks like an artist's easel!)

市 **city, market** (woman in hat holding shopping bags)

工 **construction** (looks like scaffolding or a tower)

公 **public** (八 **eight** + ム looks like a nose! Eight nosey people = the public!)

図 **drawing, map** (囗 is the **picture frame**, the inside is modern art)

魚 **fish** (components: **hook, rice field, fire**. The fish is hooked, cooked on fire, eaten with rice)

酒 **rice wine, alcohol** (**water** radical indicates liquid, right side looks like a decanter)

茶 **tea** (**vegetation** radical indicates tea leaves + umbrella shape for drinking tea under)

薬 **medicine** (**vegetation** and **tree** indicate herbal medicine;

白 (**white**) + four short strokes = aspirin dissolving!)

洗 **wash** (**water** radical on left).

Now you are going to match some common signs and shop names with their English equivalents.

a bookshop (two answers)

b a newsstand, a kiosk

c pharmacy (two answers)

d butcher's

e toilet (hand-washing)

f art gallery

g greengrocer's (800 varieties!)

h park

i fishmonger's

j market (place)

k library

l tea/coffee shop

m wine shop, liquor store

n drinking place, bar

o factory

1 公園

2 薬局

3 市場

4 図書館

5 酒屋

6 喫茶店

(focus on 2nd + 3rd 漢字)

7 売店

8 薬屋

9 書店

10 肉屋

11 飲酒店

12 美術館

13 工場

14 八百屋

15 本屋

16 魚屋

17 お手洗い

8.5 More about places

How did you get on with Activity 1? Some of the words need further explanation.

- 八百屋 (**greengrocer's**) literally means '800 shop', so think of 800 types of fruit and vegetables!

- You should have worked out the meaning of 喫茶店 (**coffee/tea shop**) from the second and third 漢字. The first one 喫 has a general meaning of eat, drink, smoke, and its radical 口 (**mouth**) indicates this general meaning. It is not widely used, and focusing on the second two 漢字 gives you the meaning.

- 工場 (**factory**) and 市場 (**market**) are both places which have grounds and so use 場 for place.

Insight

Note that お手洗い (toilet) has hiragana お (o) at the beginning, which is used in front of some words to make them sound more polite and genteel. This is sometimes translated as honourable, so in this case 'the honourable hand-washing (place)', although its real meaning is toilet! The end hiragana い is sometimes left off.

8.6 More place names

As explained in the introduction, these sections will teach additional 漢字 words which you can leave out or come back to later if you feel you have taken in enough at this stage.

The following 漢字 are key to the additional place names introduced further on:

1 主 (master) **2** 駅 (station)

3 便 (convenience; mail) **4** 行 (go)

Now let's look at them in detail.

Kanji 1

主 looks like a candlestick with a flame on top, so you can remember it as **candle** (its real meaning is **master**). It is a component of the following two 漢字:

駐 (**reside, stop-over**) 住 (**reside, dwell**)

駐 The radical is 馬 (**horse**). In old times, stop-over places or inns were a place to rest horses on a long journey. A welcoming candle in the window would light your way.

住 The radical is 人 (**person**). A person is master (real meaning of 主) in their own residence.

Places

駐車場 car park (stop-over place for vehicles)

住所 address (place of residence)

Kanji 2

駅 The radical is **horse**, the right side 尺 is the measurement **foot**. Think of it in this case as being 'R' for **railway**. *Meaning*: **railway station** (before trains, transport was by horse!)

Kanji 3

便 (**convenience; mail**). The left side is **person**, the right is 一 (one) and 曳 (tug). Here are two words it is used in – you supply the story!

Kanji 4

行 (**to go**). The radical 彳 means **going person**.

Places

銀行   (bank) 銀 means silver (radical 金 is metal). Story: Go to the bank to get silver (money).

商店街   (shopping area) You should recognize 店 (shop), 商 means trade, 街 consists of 'double earth' (土) between 行 and means street or quarters (earth piled up to make a road).

旅行案内所   (travel information) 旅行 means travel. 旅 has the left-side radical 方 which means direction, the right side comes from 衣 meaning clothes. Story: Go (行) in the direction of a holiday with a suitcase of clothes! 案内所 means information (place). Quick story for 案: tourists would certainly want more information about a woman wearing a large hat in a tree! (内 is introduced later in this unit.)

Kanji 5

More places containing 所 (**place**):

両替所 (**money exchange place**). 両 means **both**. You can see 山 (**mountain**) within this with a small mountain on **both** sides of the large one! The upper part of 替 (**exchange**) looks like two people who are **exchanging**. **Both** gain from the exchange!

精算所 (**fare adjustment office**). You learned the first 漢字 in Unit 7: it means **purity** or **white rice**. The radical means **rice**. Focus on this meaning to give you a story for the whole word. In ancient times, rice rather than money was used as payment, including fares!

Insight

If you travel by underground in Japan and do not know the fare to your destination, buy the cheapest ticket and pay the difference when you arrive, at the 精算所 – fare adjustment office.

Kanji 6

More places containing 場 (**place**):

切符売場 (**ticket office**). 売場 literally means 'selling place'. 切 means **cut** (刀 means **sword**). 符 means **token** and has 竹 (**bamboo**) at the top and 付 (**attach**) below. Maybe in ancient times a ticket was a token cut from bamboo!

劇場 (**theatre**). 劇 means **drama**. If you look hard enough, you can make out the outline of the arch and curtains around a stage with a kabuki actor standing in the middle!

Kanji 7

More places containing 館 (**hall**):

映画館 (**cinema**). Focus on 画, which means **picture** but you can also see within it four squares representing the screens of a multiscreen cinema!

旅館 (**Japanese inn**). 旅 means **travel**. A place to stay when travelling.

博物館 (**museum**). You learned 物 in Unit 4 – it means **things**. Focus on 博, meaning **PhD** or **esteem**. Esteemed items are kept in museums. Also, think of the left side of 博 as an ancient Japanese sword!

練習二 *Activity 2*

In Section 8.6, you have been introduced to 15 more place names. The following activity gives you the chance to see how many you can now recognize. If you do not get them all on the first try, simply go back over the explanations – then try again!

Match the English words (a–o) (there are clues in brackets) to the 漢字 words in the box (1–15).

- **a** travel information (*woman in tree*)
- **b** Japanese inn (*travel place*)
- **c** museum (*Japanese sword*)
- **d** theatre (*proscenium arch*)
- **e** car park (*stop-overs for horses!*)
- **f** address (*master of residence*)
- **g** fare adjustment office (*pay with rice*)
- **h** money exchange (*two people exchange*)
- **i** shopping area (*double earth for road*)
- **j** railway station (*horse + R for railway*)
- **k** ticket office (*cut bamboo selling place!*)
- **l** bank (*go to bank for silver money*)
- **m** cinema (*four squares = four screens*)

n post office (*mail bureau*)
o toilet (*convenience / your own story*)

> **1** 駐車場 (　) **2** 住所 (　) **3** 駅 (　)
> **4** 便所 (　) **5** 郵便局 (　) **6** 銀行 (　)
> **7** 商店街 (　) **8** 旅行案内所 (　) **9** 両替所 (　)
> **10** 精算所 (　) **11** 切符売場 (　) **12** 劇場 (　)
> **13** 映画館 (　) **14** 旅館 (　) **15** 博物館 (　)

8.7 Kanji signs

You have so far been exposed to a total of 47 place names (or 32 if you missed out Section 8.6). Next, you are going to learn to recognize more common signs and written information containing 漢字 or components that you are already familiar with. These are:

1 車 (*vehicle*) **2** 室 (*room*) **3** 国 (*country*)
4 席 (*seat*) **5** 物 (*thing*) **6** 料 (*fee*)

Now let us look at these in detail.

1 車 (*vehicle*). Here are five 漢字 words containing 車:

空車 *unoccupied taxi*   満車 *occupied taxi*
列車 *long-distance train*   寝台車 *sleeper train*
自転車 *bicycle*

空車 and 満車. These signs are displayed on the windscreens of taxi cabs and at car parks. 空 means **sky** or **empty** and, if you look carefully, looks like an aeroplane taking off into the air from a runway! It is also used in 空港 (**airport**).

満 means **full** or **enough**. The radical is **water**, and it contains a component you have already learned in this unit, 両 (**both**). Above this is the component vegetation. Story: Water and vegetation together are **enough** to live on!

列車. You have already learned 電車 (*electric train*). This is used generically, but also for local trains, whereas 列車 denotes long-distance trains. The right-hand component 刂 looks like a long rail track!

寝台車. 台 means **pedestal**, but can you see a person with a large nose 厶 lying on a bed? 寝 means **to sleep** and has the radical 宀 (**lid**), in this case **roof**. On the left is a component which looks like a bed standing upright – the type you pull down from the wall on a train.

自転車. You met 転 (**turn, rotate**) in Unit 7. 自 means **automatic** or **self**. You can see 目 (**eye**) with an extra short stroke. Think of this as a small nose (between the eyes!). The Japanese point to their nose (rather than their chest) when they refer to 'me'. Altogether, we have 'self-rotating vehicle', in other words, a **bicycle**!

2 室 (**room**). This is similar to 屋 (**store**), which you learned earlier in this unit (Section 8.4). The radical is different. Here, it is 宀 (**lid, roof**). The lower part is 至 (**arrive**), but focus on its difference from shop because it has a roof – 'rooms have roofs'. Here are two 漢字 words containing 室:

洋室 **Western-style room**　和室 **Japanese-style room**

洋室 and 和室 are words used in hotels and estate agents. 和室 (**Japanese-style rooms**) have tatami mats on the floor, futon mattresses to sleep on and Japanese baths, whereas 洋室

(**Western-style rooms**) have carpets on the floor and in hotels have Western beds and bathrooms.

洋 means **ocean** (the West is across the ocean!) and the radical is **water**. The right side 羊 means **sheep** (can you see the horns of the ram?), an animal associated with the West.

和 is the old Chinese word for **Japan**. You learned it as **peace** in Unit 3 (as part of the Shōwa era). The left side 禾 represents the ears of rice as it grows in the fields, and rice is Japan's staple food.

3 国 (**country**). Here are five words containing this 漢字:

国内 domestic   外国 abroad, foreign
外国爲替 foreign exchange   国際電話 international phone
入国管理 passport control

内 means **inside** (inside the country). You can see a person 人 inside a frame. (Do not confuse with 肉 **flesh** – two persons in a frame.)

外 means **outside** (outside the country). The radical 夕 means **evening** (imagine it as a crescent-moon shape) and imagine a person 卜 standing outside looking at the moon. 外国人 means **foreigner** (outsider). 外国爲替 contains 替 meaning **exchange** (see *Kanji 5* in Section 8.6).

国際電話. You learned 電話 (**telephone**) in Unit 6. 際 is used to indicate **international** and consists of the radical **village** (think of the global village) and 祭 meaning **festival**. (Think of the upper part being a marquee and the lower part a trestle table, set up for a fête or festival.)

入国管理. First, you have **enter the country** (to enter a country you have to show your passport). Focus then on 管. You learned in Section 8.4 (part 6) that the component 官 means

government, and passport control is a government or civil service organization.

4 席 (**seat**). The radical is 广 (**dotted cliff**), but for this 漢字, imagine it is the roof and side of a train carriage (with electric cable on the roof). The component within looks like a computer game character! He has a square head, stick body and arms. You cannot see his legs because he is sitting down! Here are two signs containing 席:

自由席 unreserved seat   指定席 reserved seat

You have already learned that 自 means **self**. 自由 means **freedom** – the freedom to make your own (self) decisions. With 席, it means **free/unreserved seat**.

指 means **finger/indicate**. The general meaning is indicated by the left-hand radical **hand** (from 手). 定 means **fixed**. The general meaning (putting a limit on something) is indicated by the radical 宀 (a crown or, in this case, a **lid**). Therefore the seats indicated are limited/reserved.

Note: 定食 means **set meal** (in other words, the menu is **fixed**).

5 物 (**thing**). You first learned this in Unit 4 (Section 4.5).

荷物 luggage, parcel
忘れ物 left behind by mistake/lost luggage

Look at 荷 as a picture of a suitcase (口) coming through the conveyor belt at the airport! 忘 means **forgotten**. Remember that the radical 心 (**heart**) is used for emotions and thoughts. 亡 means **deceased** or **lost**.

6 料 (**fee**). Focus on the radical 米 (**rice**), which you know can represent payment:

料金　means **fee** (*lit.* 'fee money')

入場料　means **entrance fee** (*lit.* 'enter place fee')

無料　means **admission free** (*lit.* 'no fee'). 無 means **nothing** and looks like a prison window with **no** prisoner inside!

練習三 *Activity 3*

In the last section, you were introduced to 22 new information words and three new general 漢字 (室、席、料). Test yourself by seeing how many you can recognize (write the English meanings in the brackets). If you cannot remember all of them at first, check your answers by looking back through the section.

空車 (　　) 満車 (　　　) 列車 (　　　) 寝台車 (　　　)

自転車 (　　) 洋室 (　　　) 和室 (　　　) 国内 (　　　)

外国 (　　) 外国人 (　　　) 外国爲替 (　　　)

国際電話 (　　) 入国管理 (　　　) 祭 (　　　)

自由席 (　　) 指定席 (　　　) 定食 (　　) 荷物 (　　　)

忘れ物 (　　) 料金 (　　) 入場料 (　　　) 無料 (　　　)

8.8 More signs

As with Section 8.6, you can leave this one out and come back to it later if you wish to.

1 Here are three compound words containing 室 (room):

浴室 bathroom　　　　　　化粧室 powder room, toilet

待合室 waiting room

浴室. 浴 means **bathe** and has the **water** radical on the left. The right-hand component looks like a house, as in 'bath house'!

Insight

The word for a Japanese-style bath is 風呂. This type of bath is deeper and shorter than Western baths, and you sit with your knees bent and only your head above water. 呂 means backbone (can you see the vertebrae?) – you sit in the bath with your back straight.

化粧室. 化粧 means **cosmetics** (think of the rice radical 米 as a powder puff!). **Powder room** is a euphemism for ladies' toilet or bathroom.

待合室. Focus on 待, which means **wait**. The left-hand radical is **going person** and the right-hand radical is 寺 (**temple**).

2 In Section 8.7, you learned 和 (**Japanese**) and 洋 (**Western**). Here are four more words containing these:

和食 Japanese cuisine   洋食 Western cuisine
和式 Japanese-style   洋式 Western-style

練習四 Activity 4

In Section 8.8, you have been introduced to eight new compound words (1–8). Can you match them up with their English meanings (a–h)?

1 和食   **a** Western-style
2 和式   **b** Japanese-style
3 待合室   **c** Western cuisine

4 浴室　　　　　**d** Japanese cuisine

5 風呂　　　　　**e** bathroom

6 化粧室　　　　**f** (Japanese) bath

7 洋食　　　　　**g** waiting room

8 洋式　　　　　**h** powder room (ladies' toilet)

8.9 A map of Japan

In this section, you will learn to recognize the main islands and cities of Japan. First, you are going to learn the four compass directions:

And here are quick clues to help you remember them:

北　**north** (looks like two people sitting back to back to keep warm (cold in the North))

南　**south** (yen symbol ¥ (more money in the South of Japan!))

東　**east** (components: **sun** and **tree**. Sun rising in the east from behind the tree)

西　**west** (looks like 四 **four** (do not confuse them) – it is the fourth compass direction)

Now look at the map of Japan on the following page with the main islands and cities labelled in 漢字 and rōmaji. How many 漢字 do you recognize? There is a list of clues to help you learn the names. You have not learned any of the 漢字 for 3, 6 and 12. They are included for interest only.

漢字

	Place	漢字 Meanings	Story clue
1	日本	sun, root	'Land of the rising sun'
2	北海道	North, sea, way	'North island across the sea'
3	札幌	paper money, hood	Winter Olympics held here – brought in money!
4	本州	root/main, province	Main (biggest) island of Japan
5	東京	East, capital	(Which it is!)
6	横浜	side, seacoast	'City on the seacoast to the side of Tokyo'
7	大阪	big, slope	Osaka is built on a hillside.
8	京都	capital, city	Kyoto used to be the capital of Japan.

9 広島	wide, island	Hiroshima stands in a wide bay dotted with small islands.
10 四国	four, country	Shikoku is the fourth of the main islands of Japan.
11 九州	nine, province	Kyushu is divided into nine provinces (administrative).
12 長崎	long, promontory	Describes Nagasaki harbour.

8.10 Warning signs

It is very useful – and often essential – to be able to read this type of sign. A friend of mine drove up a closed road and got stuck in a snow drift because she could not read the sign at the head of the road. After that, she learned to recognize 禁 (**forbidden**) as 'two Harry Worths (the entertainer who used to stand half behind mirrors lifting his leg and arm up and down) dancing on a picnic table'! That 漢字 alone would have prevented her going up that road.

We start by learning some general warning 漢字 then look at how they are used.

禁 forbidden (just mentioned)
禁止 **no, not allowed** (止 means **stop**)
厳禁 **strictly forbidden** 煙 **to smoke** (**fire** radical)
中 **middle**. In signs means **during** or **under**

練習五 Activity 5

Here are some common warning signs using the 漢字 we have just met, plus ones you know already.

Match each word (1–5) to its English meaning (a–e).

1 駐車禁止	**a** Outdoor shoes strictly forbidden ( )
2 立入禁止	**b** No smoking ( )
3 禁煙	**c** No parking ( )
4 土足厳禁	**d** Under construction ( )
5 工事中	**e** No admittance ( )

Finally in this section, three more useful warning signs with clues to remember:

非常口	**Emergency exit** (非 looks like a path cleared of clutter for easy access)
注意	**Caution** (注 *Story*: 'Pour water on a candle to caution against fire'!)
危険	**Danger** (危 looks like a snake in a box – dangerous if it escapes!)

8.11 Pairs of signs

Ten 漢字 follow which can be paired as opposites in meaning.

左 *left*	Use of 工 for **I** (am/am not left handed)
右 *right*	口 ('Tick the **right** box')
押す *push*	Hand radical is **pushing** the doorbell.
引く *pull*	引 looks like an archery bow which you **pull**.

開 *open*	Gates (elevator doors). Two people holding one door each **open**.
閉 *close*	One person cannot hold the doors, and they close.
到着 *arrival*	Remember that 至 means **arrive** or 'the nose of the plane touching ground'.
出発 *departure*	出 means **go out**.
営業中 *open for business*	営 is a backbone with a hat on – a shop assistant!
休業中 *closed*	休 means **holiday**.

8.12 Miscellaneous signs

And finally, some miscellaneous signs. Once more, you can miss this section out if you need to consolidate what you have learned so far.

焼 means **grilled** (**fire** radical plus component looking like a barbecue). Look at these words:

焼肉	*yakiniku* – grilled meat
焼き鳥	*yakitori* – barbecued chicken on bamboo skewers
お好み焼き	*okonomiyaki* – a type of thick pancake cooked on an iron griddle at your table
すき焼き	*sukiyaki* – beef grilled, then cooked with vegetables in a cast-iron pot
新幹線	*shinkansen* or bullet train. 新 (**new**) helps you to remember this
地下鉄	*underground* (train). *Lit*: 'ground under iron'. Iron indicates the rail track.
急行	*express* (train). *Lit*: 'hurry go'
特急	*special express*. *Lit*: 'special hurry'

練習六 *Activity 6*

Look at the pictures of various Japanese signs. There is a range of written styles, both vertical and horizontal left to right. How many can you recognize?

Insight

You may need to come back to this activity after you have worked through the conclusion (which includes a review of all the signs learned in this unit) – but keep a score and see if you can improve on it!

1

2

3

4

The name of a temple entrance

5

6

7

南口

8

北口

9

10

11

下北沢駅

SHIMOKITAZAWA

What is Shimokitazawa the name of? (Focus on the last *kanji*)

12

富士銀行

The first two *kanji* mean Fuji. What is this building called?

13

営業時間

14 国際電話

15 自由

16 空車

17 和室

18 立入禁止

19 禁煙

8.13 終りに Conclusion

おめでとう (*omedetō*) Congratulations! You have worked through a minimum of 76 漢字 signs in this unit. This does not include the 12 island and city names, and the 31 signs in Sections 8.4, 8.6 and 8.8. This makes an overall total of 119 signs, which is a huge amount – obviously you are not going to remember them all in one go.

8.14 テスト Test yourself

To help you review and consolidate your learning, all the signs are grouped below by theme. How many do you remember? The English is also given at the end of the unit, so test yourself, then check and use these pages as a check list. (Signs taught in Sections 8.4, 8.6 and 8.8 are marked with an asterisk.)

Insight

To help you remember kanji words, try writing them out on small squares of card. Put the 漢字 on one side and the English on the other. Use these mini flashcards to test yourself by looking at the 漢字 side, giving your answer then turning the card over to see if you are right. Try doing ten in the morning, ten in the evening and gradually build up the number you can remember.

General

1 出口	**2** 入口	**3** 女	**4** 男
5 大人	**6** 小人	**7** お手洗い	**8** 便所*
9 化粧室	**10** 左	**11** 右	**12** 和式*
13 洋式*			

Shopping and places in town

1 店	**2** 肉屋	**3** 八百屋	**4** 本屋
5 魚屋	**6** 酒屋	**7** 喫茶店	**8** 飲酒店
9 書店	**10** 売店	**11** 薬局	**12** 薬屋
13 市場	**14** 公園	**15** 図書館	**16** 商店街*
17 国際電話	**18** 銀行*	**19** 郵便局*	**20** 外国爲替
21 両替所*	**22** 駐車場*	**23** 押す	**24** 引く
25 開	**26** 閉	**27** 営業中	**28** 休業中
29 工場	**30** 学校		

Sightseeing and entertainment

1 美術館	2 お寺	3 休日	4 祭
5 映画館*	6 博物館*	7 劇場*	8 料金
9 入場料	10 無料		

Travel and transport

1 北	2 南	3 東
4 西	5 外国人	6 到着
7 出発	8 入国管理	9 国内
10 駅*	11 電車	12 上り
13 下り	14 列車	15 寝台車
16 自由席	17 指定席	18 荷物
19 忘れ物	20 精算所*	21 切符売場*
22 旅行案内所*	23 新幹線*	24 急行*
25 特急*	26 地下鉄*	27 空車
28 満車	29 自転車	30 待合室*

Accommodation

1 旅館*	2 洋室	3 和室
4 浴室*	5 風呂*	6 住所*

Warnings

1 駐車禁止	2 立入禁止	3 禁煙	4 土足厳禁
5 工事中	6 非常口	7 注意	8 危険

Food and drink

1 和食*	2 洋食*	3 焼肉*
4 焼き鳥*	5 お好み焼き*	6 すき焼き*

English meanings

General

1 exit   **2** entrance   **3** woman
4 man   **5** adult   **6** child
7 toilet   **8** toilet   **9** toilet/powder room
10 left   **11** right   **12** Japanese-style
13 Western-style

Shopping and places in town

1 shop   **2** butcher
3 greengrocer   **4** bookshop
5 fish shop   **6** liquor store
7 coffee shop   **8** bar
9 bookstore   **10** kiosk
11 and **12** pharmacy/chemist's   **13** market
14 park   **15** library
16 shopping area   **17** international telephone
18 bank   **19** post office
20 foreign exchange   **21** exchange bureau
22 car park   **23** push
24 pull   **25** open
26 close   **27** open (for business)
28 closed   **29** factory
30 school

Sightseeing and entertainment

1 art gallery   **2** temple   **3** holiday   **4** festival
5 cinema   **6** museum   **7** theatre   **8** fee
9 entrance fee   **10** admission free

Travel and transport

1 north   **2** south
3 east   **4** west

5 foreigner
7 departure
9 domestic
11 train
13 down
15 sleeper
17 reserved seat
19 lost property
21 ticket office
23 bullet train
25 special express
27 unoccupied (taxi)
29 bicycle

6 arrival
8 passport control
10 station
12 up
14 long-distance train
16 unreserved seat
18 luggage
20 fare adjustment office
22 travel information
24 express
26 underground/subway
28 occupied (taxi)
30 waiting room

Accommodation

1 Japanese inn
3 Japanese-style room
5 (Japanese) bath

2 Western-style room
4 bathroom
6 address

Warnings

1 no parking
3 no smoking
5 under construction
7 caution

2 no admittance
4 outdoor shoes strictly forbidden
6 emergency exit
8 danger

Food and drink

1 Japanese cuisine
3 *yakiniku* – grilled meat
5 *okonomiyaki* – grilled pancake

2 Western cuisine
4 *yakitori* – grilled chicken
6 *sukiyaki* – beef 'hot pot'

9

第九課
Unit 9

In this unit, you will:
- *learn to read the 46 カタカナ (katakana) symbols which make up the phonetic 'alphabet'*
- *learn some rules for making extra sounds from the 46 main symbols*
- *be introduced to picture–sound associations to make learning easier*
- *learn how to write カタカナ (katakana)*
- *have a go at reading some words and phrases*

9.1 はじめに Introduction

カタカナ (*katakana*) is the script used to represent foreign words which have been adopted into the Japanese language (loan words) and foreign names (personal names, countries, etc.). Most of the loan words are derived from English words, and this means that once you can read the script, you can normally work out what a word means. This makes カタカナ a fun script to learn, and working out the meanings can be an enjoyable challenge!

In Unit 5, you learned to read the ひらがな script. You may have decided to work through the 漢字 units first and then to work on Units 5 and 9. And you could work through this unit without learning ひらがな first, but as most of the rules are the same for both scripts, you will be referred back to the appropriate section in Unit 5 to read through the explanations there.

Begin by looking back to the **Only got five minutes?** section at the start of book, which deals with an overview of the different types of Japanese script and has a paragraph on カタカナ. Can you answer these questions based on the information you have just read?

1 What is カタカナ used for? (name four uses)
2 What do カタカナ symbols originate from?
3 How many basic symbols make up the カタカナ syllabary?

9.2 Work it out!

You have not learned to read any カタカナ yet (apart from these three symbols), but as you did in Unit 5, you are going to pair up カタカナ words which are the same. There are six words (a–f) in the left column which are repeated in a different order in the right column. Match up the same words and write the correct letter in the brackets on the right. The first one is done for you.

a ケーキ   スカート ( )
b アイス   ステーキ ( )
c トースト   ケーキ (a)
d ステーキ   スーツ ( )
e スカート   アイス ( )
f スーツ   トースト ( )

9.3 How to read katakana

Let us begin by looking at the first four lines of the カタカナ syllabary with the romanized pronunciation and learn how to read them. The order and pronunciation is exactly the same as ひらがな (see Section 5.3 to refresh your memory). Only the symbols are different. The chart is written in the traditional way from top to bottom right to left. This is to give you practice at reading vertically.

Insight

Remember that you read in columns not rows and begin to read from the top right symbol.

ta タ	sa サ	ka カ	a ア
chi チ	shi シ	ki キ	i イ
tsu ツ	su ス	ku ク	u ウ
te テ	se セ	ke ケ	e エ
to ト	so ソ	ko コ	o オ

練習一 *Activity 1*

In the Work it out! activity, you matched six カタカナ words. Now you are going to try to read those words. Use the chart of the first 20 symbols above and say the words out loud. Then see if you can match them to their English meanings in the box that follows. Remember that カタカナ is used to write foreign (mainly English) words. The pronunciation is adapted to suit Japanese pronunciation rules (every consonant is followed by a vowel), but you can usually recognize the word once you have read it correctly.

Insight

A dash ー after a symbol means that you lengthen the sound of that symbol. (う [u] performs this function in ひらがな. See the note below Activity 4 in Section 5.5).

a ケーキ	**b** トースト	**c** ステーキ
d アイス	**e** スカート	**f** スーツ

skirt ( )	suit ( )	steak ( )
cake ( )	ice ( )	toast ( )

In Unit 5, you were introduced to the idea of remembering ひらがな through visual and sound association (Section 5.4). Here are a few ideas for カタカナ symbols to get you started. Try to think of your own and write them down. Some symbols are easier than others, but just do a few at a time.

ア (a) looks like an antelope

イ (i) is a leaning T which rhymes with i

ウ (u) looks like a uisukiī (whisky) flask

エ (e) looks like elevator doors

キ (ki) looks like a door key

9.4 The katakana chart

You are now going to be introduced to the whole カタカナ chart, including the correct order in which to write each symbol. This follows exactly the same format as for ひらがな in Unit 5 (Section 5.4).

As with ひらがな, try to learn to write カタカナ, because this will help you to remember how to read them, too. Look carefully at the stroke order and remember that, in general, you write horizontal strokes from left to right and vertical/diagonal strokes from top to bottom (variations to the direction are marked with an arrow on the individual symbol).

ナ na	タ ta	サ sa	カ ka	ア a
ナ	タ	サ	カ	ア
一 ナ	ノ ク タ	一 十 サ	フ カ	丶 ア
ニ ni	**チ chi**	**シ shi**	**キ ki**	**イ i**
ニ	チ	シ	キ	イ
一 ニ	ノ 二 チ	丶 ニ シ	一 二 キ	ノ イ
ヌ nu	**ツ tsu**	**ス su**	**ク ku**	**ウ u**
ヌ	ツ	ス	ク	ウ
フ ヌ	丶 丶 ツ	フ ス	ノ ク	丶 丶 ウ
ネ ne	**テ te**	**セ se**	**ケ ke**	**エ e**
ネ	テ	セ	ケ	エ
丶 フ ネ ネ	一 二 テ	フ セ	ノ ト ケ	一 丁 エ
ノ no	**ト to**	**ソ so**	**コ ko**	**オ o**
ノ	ト	ソ	コ	オ
ノ	l ト	丶 ソ	フ コ	一 十 オ

Insight
Organize your learning

Don't worry about learning all the symbols in one go – keep referring back to the charts.

You might find it useful to make a カタカナ vocabulary book for this unit. You could either organize the words by theme (food, drink, clothes, electrical gadgets, etc.) or alphabetically using the 46 basic symbols (one per page) and enter all words beginning with a particular symbol on the same page. Whichever way you choose, write out each カタカナ word with its rōmaji pronunciation (optional) and its English meaning next to it. You can then test yourself by covering up the English and seeing if you can read the カタカナ word. And it will form a useful dictionary too!

練習二 Activity 2

Now that you have been introduced to the 46 カタカナ symbols, it is time to put your learning into practice and have a go at reading some words. As in Unit 5, the words are in three sets. Set 1 refers to the first part of the chart, set 2 refers to the second and set 3 to the whole chart. You also have to select the correct English meanings, so say the words out loud. You may be able to do this, even if you cannot read all the かな (kana) symbols. See how many symbols/words you can read from memory before using the chart to search for those you cannot remember. Keep coming back to this activity and try to improve your score each time!

Insight
Pronunciation of r and l

Japanese pronunciation does not distinguish between r and l sounds. Try replacing r sounds with l sounds if you cannot work out the meaning. For example, ランチ (ranchi) means lunch.

Set 1

a ケーキ   **b** ココア   **c** タクシー   **d** コート
e セーター   **f** スキー   **g** スケート

1 skating ( )   **2** skiing ( )   **3** cocoa ( )   **4** taxi ( )
5 cake ( )   **6** sweater ( )   **7** coat ( )

Set 2

a ラーメン   **b** ハム   **c** メモ
d メロン   **e** レモン

1 memo ( )   **2** lemon ( )   **3** melon ( )
4 ham ( )   **5** rāmen (Chinese noodles) ( )

Set 3

a チキン   **b** アイスクリーム   **c** カレー
d ライス   **e** トマト   **f** レストラン
g テニス   **h** カメラ

1 restaurant ( ) **2** tennis ( ) **3** rice ( )
4 chicken ( ) **5** curry ( ) **6** ice cream ( )
7 camera ( ) **8** tomato ( )

....

Insight
Similar katakana

You have probably already confused some of the similar-looking カタカナ. This section will line these up so that you can look at the differences and keep them separate in your mind.

ア、マ (a, ma)　　　　　サ、セ (sa, se)
ク、タ、ヌ (ku, ta, nu)　ウ、フ、ワ (u, fu, wa)
ナ、メ (na, me)　　　　　ル、レ (ru, re)
シ、ツ (shi, tsu)

- The long stroke in シ is written upwards (like a tick), and the short strokes are almost at right angles to the long stroke.
- The long stroke in ツ is written downwards and is at a steeper angle. The short strokes stand side by side.

ン、ソ (n, so)

- ン has the same features as シ, and ソ has the same features as ツ (but each only has one short stroke).

....

....

Insight
Similar hiragana and katakana

The good news is that some カタカナ symbols are very similar to their ひらがな equivalents (in many cases, they originated from the same 漢字). This can make them easier to remember. They are listed here, ひらがな first, then カタカナ:

う、ウ (u)	か、カ (ka)	き、キ (ki)
け、ケ (ke)	こ、コ (ko)	せ、セ (se)
に、ニ (ni)	へ、ヘ (he)	も、モ (mo)
や、ヤ (ya)	り、リ (ri)	

9.5 Katakana that change their sound

Again, the rules are exactly the same as for ひらがな, only the script is different. Read over the ひらがな section again (Section 5.6), then fill in the gaps in the following activity. And remember, just as with all the units in this book, you set the pace!

練習三 *Activity 3*

When you add ゛ (*ten ten*) to certain symbols, you get a change in sound.

1 k sounds become g sounds (hard g as in **get**):

カ、 キ、 ク、 ケ、 コ → ガ、ギ、グ、ゲ、ゴ
(*ka*) (*ki*) (*ku*) (*ke*) (*ko*) ( ) ( ) ( ) ( ) ( )

2 s sounds → z sounds:

サ、 シ、 ス、 セ、 ソ → ザ、ジ、ズ、ゼ、ゾ
(*sa*) (*shi*) (*su*) (*se*) (*so*) ( ) ( )* ( ) ( ) ( )

3 t sounds become d sounds:

タ、 テ、 ト → ダ、 デ、 ド
(*ta*) (*te*) (*to*) ( ) ( ) ( )

4 h sounds become b sounds:

ハ、 ヒ、 フ、 ヘ、 ホ → バ、 ビ、 ブ、 ベ、 ボ
(*ha*) (*hi*) (*fu*) (*he*) (*ho*) ( ) ( ) ( ) ( ) ( )

5 In addition, **h** sounds become **p** sounds when a small circle ° is added:

ハ、ヒ、フ、へ、ホ → パ、ピ、プ、ペ、ポ
(*ha*) (*hi*) (*fu*) (*he*) (*ho*)   ( ) ( ) ( ) ( ) ( )

Check whether you have filled in the brackets correctly by referring back to this section in Unit 5 (Section 5.6).

練習四 *Activity 4*

This activity is designed to help you build up your confidence in reading カタカナ and to ease you away from referring back to the charts (but they are always there if you need them!). This will be done by re-introducing a few カタカナ symbols at a time and getting you to read words which contain them. Section by section, you will build up the number of symbols until you are reading words containing them all. For each section, look over the カタカナ symbols, then match up the words and meanings beneath them. When a symbol has linked sounds (for example, カ (*ka*)、ガ (*ga*)), they are given together, but not all are necessarily used in that section.

1 サ (sa)、ザ (za)、シ (shi)、ジ (ji)、ス (su)、ズ (zu)、
チ (chi)、テ (te)、デ (de)、ト (to)、ド (do)、ン (n)

a トースト   **b** デザート   **c** チーズ
d ジーンズ   **e** シーン

i jeans ( )   **ii** cheese ( )   **iii** toast ( )
iv (movie) scene ( )   **v** dessert ( )

2 カ (ka)、ガ (ga)、セ (se)、ゼ (ze)、ソ (so)、
ゾ (zo)、ツ (tsu)、ハ (ha)、バ (ba)、パ (pa)

a ソーセージ　**b** ハンバーガー　**c** パンツ
d バス　　　　　**e** スカート

  i pants/trousers ( )　　**ii** skirt ( )　　　**iii** sausage ( )
iv bus or bath ( )　　**v** hamburger ( )

3 | コ (ko)、ゴ (go)、タ (ta)、ダ (da)、ヒ (hi)、
　ビ (bi)、ピ (pi)、フ (fu)、ブ (bu)、プ (pu)

  a スカーフ　**b** テープ　**c** ピザ　　　**d** パブ
e ヒーター　**f** タバコ　**g** ダンス

  i tobacco (cigarettes) ( )　　**ii** (sticky or video) tape ( )
iii heater ( )　　　　　　　**iv** pub ( )
 v scarf ( )　　　　　　　　**vi** pizza ( )
vii dance ( )

4 | キ (ki)、ギ (gi)、ケ (ke)、ゲ (ge)、ヘ (he)、
　ベ (be)、ペ (pe)、ホ (ho)、ボ (bo)、ポ (po)

  a チキン　　**b** ギター　　　**c** パスポート
d ペン　　　**e** スーツケース　**f** ボタン
g ベンチ

  i passport ( )　　**ii** suitcase ( )　　**iii** chicken ( )
iv pen ( )　　　**v** bench ( )　　　**vi** guitar ( )
vii button ( )

5 | ラ (ra)、リ (ri)、ル* (ru)、レ (re)、ロ (ro)
　(l or r sound can be used for these)

Insight
ル is often used as the final l sound, for example, ホテル
(hotel)、プール (pool).

a サラダ   **b** カレー   **c** レンタカー
d レストラン   **e** フロント   **f** アイスリンク
g テーブル   **h** ダブル   **i** ゴルフ
j ビール   **k** セール   **l** ベースボール

i table ( )   **ii** curry ( )
iii golf ( )   **iv** front (reception) ( )
v beer ( )   **vi** salad ( )
vii sale ( )   **viii** double ( )
ix ice rink ( )   **x** baseball ( )
xi rental car ( )   **xii** restaurant ( )

6 ク (ku)、グ (gu)、マ (ma)、ミ (mi)、ム (mu)、メ (me)、モ (mo)

a トマト   **b** ミルク   **c** ハム
d カメラ   **e** グラム   **f** モカ

i tomato ( )   **ii** ham ( )   **iii** gram ( )
iv camera ( )   **v** mocha (coffee) ( )   **vi** milk ( )

7 ナ (na)、ニ (ni)、ヌ (nu)、ネ (ne)、ノ (no)

a バナナ   **b** テニス   **c** ネクタイ
d ノート   **e** カヌー

i tennis ( )   **ii** canoe ( )   **iii** banana ( )
iv necktie ( )   **v** note(book) ( )

8 ア (a)、イ (i)、ウ (u)、エ (e)、オ (o)、ワ (wa)

a アイスクリーム   **b** ブラウス
c エスカレーター   **d** ステレオ   **e** ワイン

i ice cream ( ) ii escalator ( ) iii wine ( )
iv stereo ( ) v blouse ( )

___

9.6 Contracted sounds

The only three symbols you did not use in the last activity were
ヤ、ユ、ヨ (*ya, yu, yo*). These are used as normal symbols, but
also are used to form contracted sounds. You learned about these
for ひらがな in Unit 5. The rules are the same for カタカナ.
Read back over Section 5.5 to remind or familiarize yourself with
the rules before trying the next activity.

練習五 *Activity 5*

Write the pronunciation of the contracted カタカナ sounds in the
brackets. The first line has been done for you.

キ (*ki*)	→	キャ (kya)	キュ (kyu)	キョ (kyo)
ギ (*gi*)	→	キャ ( )	ギュ ( )	ギョ ( )
シ (*shi*)	→	シャ ( )	シュ ( )	ショ ( )
ジ (*ji*)	→	ジャ ( )	ジュ ( )	ジョ ( )
チ (*chi*)	→	チャ ( )	チュ ( )	チョ ( )
ニ (*ni*)	→	ニャ ( )	ニュ ( )	ニョ ( )
ヒ (*hi*)	→	ヒャ ( )	ヒュ ( )	ヒョ ( )
ビ (*bi*)	→	ビャ ( )	ビュ ( )	ビョ ( )
ピ (*pi*)	→	ピャ ( )	ピュ ( )	ピョ ( )
ミ (*mi*)	→	ミャ ( )	ミュ ( )	ミョ ( )
リ (*ri*)	→	リャ ( )	リュ ( )	リョ ( )

Now check your answers with the equivalent charts in Unit 5
(Sections 5.5 and 5.6).

練習六 *Activity 6*

Now let us put into practice what you have learned above. Match the カタカナ words in the left column (a–j) to their English meanings on the right (1–10).

a キャンプ

b シャワー

c ジャム

d ジュース

e ジョギング

f チョコレート

g メニュー

h コンピュータ

i ミュージカル

j コミュニケーション

1 computer ( )

2 communication ( )

3 camp(ing) ( )

4 jam ( )

5 musical ( )

6 menu ( )

7 shower ( )

8 jogging ( )

9 chocolate ( )

10 juice ( )

9.7 The small ツ (tsu)

This was introduced for ひらがな in Unit 5 (Section 5.7). When you see a small ツ (tsu) in a word, you do not pronounce it, but pause slightly (a glottal stop) before saying the next sound. In カタカナ words, this has the effect of 'holding back' the next sound so that it becomes closer in pronunciation to the original word or at least easier for the Japanese to pronounce. An example will make this clearer:

ホットドッグ (**hotdog**) is pronounced *hot(to)dog(gu)*

The pronunciation of *to* and *gu* is 'held back' (and written here in brackets).

練習七 *Activity 7*

Match the カタカナ words (a–j) with their English meanings (1–10).

a カップ

b サンドイッチ

c ミックス

d サッカー

e ホッケー

f マッチ

g コインロッカー

h バスケットボール

i トイレットペーパー

j ジャケット

1 toilet paper ( )

2 coin locker ( )

3 jacket ( )

4 cup ( )

5 hockey ( )

6 soccer (football) ( )

7 sandwich ( )

8 mix ( )

9 match ( )

10 basketball ( )

9.8 Extra katakana sounds

You learned in the introduction that there are a number of uses of カタカナ, but this unit focuses on the two main uses of カタカナ:

1 to represent foreign words adopted into the Japanese language (loan words);
2 to represent foreign names (cities, countries, personal names, designer and brand names).

Insight

Not every sound in a foreign language has an equivalent sound in Japanese and, as you will have noticed already, this leads to changes in pronunciation when the word is adapted to Japanese. Some of these changes have already been pointed out. The following section deals with the rest.

1 **th** sound. This sound does not exist in Japanese, so is replaced by **s** sounds.

マラソン *ma ra so n* (**marathon**)

サッチャー *sa t chā* (**Thatcher**)

スミス *su mi su* (**Smith**)

マシュー *ma shū* (**Matthew**)

si also does not exist and is replaced with シ (*shi*) or ジ (*ji*).

シドニー *shi do nī* (**Sydney**)

ビジネス *bi ji ne su* (**business**)

2 **er** sound. This is replaced by a lengthened **a** sound (using ー).

ハンバーガー *ha n bā gā* (**hamburger**)

ピーター *pī tā* (**Peter**)

3 Some **f** sounds are replaced with **h** sounds.

テレホンカード *te re ho n kā do* (**telephone card**)

コーヒー *kō hī* (**coffee**)

4 **v** sound. This sound does not exist naturally in Japanese, the nearest equivalent being a **b** sound.

エレベーター *e re bē tā* (**elevator**)

バレーボール *ba rē bō ru* (**volleyball**)

ビデオ *bi de o* (**video**)

ラブホテル *ra bu ho te ru* (**Love Hotel**)

There also exists a group of sounds which have been designed to represent **v** sounds:

ヴァ (*va*)　ヴィ (*vi*)　ヴ (*vu*)　ヴェ (*ve*)　ヴォ (*vo*)

The rule is that these are used in foreign names and countries, but rules are often broken! Foreign names and countries are also written using the **b** sounds; other loan words are sometimes written using the **v** sounds:

ヴィクトリア *vi ku to ri a* (**Victoria**)   or

ビクトリア *bi ku to ri a*

ヴァイオリン *va i o ri n* (**violin**)   or

バイオリン *ba i o ri n*

5 **w** sounds are formed in two ways:

version 1 ウイ (*ui*)、ウエ (*ue*)、ウオ (*uo*)

version 2 ウィ (*wi*)、ウェ (*we*)、ウォ (*wo*)

In version 2, the second symbol is small.

version 1 ウイスキー *u i su kī* (**whisky**)

ウエター *u e tā* (**waiter**)

version 2 ノルウェー *no ru wē* (**Norway**)

ウォークマン *wō ku ma n* (**walkman**)

Insight

Traditionally, version 1 is used for loan words and version 2 is used for foreign names and countries. However, as with v and b (point 4 above), in practice this is not a hard-and-fast rule. It has become very fashionable to use the small symbols, and young people in particular tend to use them.

6 Combination sounds using small ア (*a*), イ (*i*), ウ (*u*), エ (*e*), オ (*o*):

In points **4** and **5** above, these are used in forming **v** and **w** sounds. They are also used to make a number of other sounds which do not exist in Japanese but are needed for foreign words. They are easy to read if you remember that the vowel part of the first symbol is replaced with the vowel sound of the small symbol. For example:

フア (*fa*)　the **u** sound of フ (*fu*) is replaced with ア (*a*)

Now you work out these sounds:

フィ ( )　　フェ ( )　　フォ ( )　　シェ ( )
ジェ ( )　　チェ ( )　　ツァ ( )　　ツェ ( )
ティ ( )　　ディ ( )

There are a few other sounds such as クァ (*kwa*), グァ (*gwa*) and クォ (*kwo*), but these are not used very often. Here are the sounds you should have written/worked out in the previous paragraph:

フィ (*fi*)　　フェ (*fe*)　　フォ (*fo*)　　シェ (*she*)
ジェ (*je*)　　チェ (*che*)　　ツァ (*tsa*)　　ツェ (*tse*)
ティ (*ti*)　　ディ (*di*)*

* Sometimes this sound is represented by ジ (*ji*) ラジオ *ra ji o* (**radio**).

練習八 *Activity 8*

This activity is designed so that you can practise reading words which contain the extra sounds you have just learned (Rules 1–6). Match the words:

a スパゲッティ　　　　**1** earphone(s) ( )

b チェックイン　　　　**2** check-in (counter) ( )

c ミルクシェイク　　　**3** fax ( )

d ミルクティー　　　　**4** spaghetti ( )

e	ウエートレス	5	disco ( )
f	フィルム	6	Sweden ( )
g	イヤホーン	7	fork ( )
h	ファックス	8	waitress ( )
i	フォーク	9	milk shake ( )
j	シルバーシート	10	milk tea ( )
k	スウェーデン	11	(camera) film ( )
l	ディスコ	12	silver seat (seats for elderly/ disabled)

9.9 Contracted words

You're nearly there – after this section, you will be ready to put your learning into real practice! Loan words adopted into any language often change pronunciation either to fit that language or because that is the way the word is heard. Take the word Japan, for example, which actually is sounded *Nihon* or *Nippon* in Japanese but was heard as **Japan** by early European travellers. You have already seen the ways that loan words are adapted to fit Japanese pronunciation rules. One final way in which loan words are adapted is by shortening or contracting them. You have already met some examples of shortened words:

ノート (*nōto*) **notebook** (the **book** part is no longer part of the word)

Other examples of shortened words are:

テレビ (*terebi*) **television** (**sion** is missing; **vi** is pronounced **bi**)

They can sometimes take on new or specific meanings:

サンド (*sando*) **toasted sandwich**
ハムサンド (*hamu sando*) **toasted ham sandwich**

> **Insight**
> The word サンド (sando) is a shortened version of
> サンドイッチ (sandoitchi – sandwich). This word is
> increasingly written with a small イ: サンドィッチ is
> used increasingly, as you learned in point 5 of Section 9.8.

Examples of contracted words are:

ディジカメ (*dijikame*) means **digi(tal) came(ra)** (missing parts in brackets)
マスコミ (*masukomi*) means **mass comm(unication)** or **mass media**

These types of words can cause the most confusion when you are trying to work out meanings, but practice makes perfect! So try the matching activity that follows.

練習九 *Activity 9*

Match the カタカナ words in the left column to their rōmaji and English equivalents and write the appropriate letters in the brackets.

1 オートバイ	( )	**a** *toire*	**i**	supermarket
2 トイレ	( )	**b** *waishatsu*	**ii**	word processor
3 ワンピース	( )	**c** *wanpīsu*	**iii**	personal computer
4 ワープロ	( )	**d** *hōmu*	**iv**	department store
5 パソコン	( )	**e** *ōtobai*	**v**	one piece (= dress)

6 ファミコン	( )	**f**	*sūpā*	**vi**	white shirt
7 ホーム	( )	**g**	*wāpuro*	**vii**	(plat)form
8 デパート	( )	**h**	*famikon*	**viii**	autobike (= motorbike)
9 スーパー	( )	**i**	*pasokon*	**ix**	toilet
10 ワイシャツ	( )	**j**	*depāto*	**x**	family computer

9.10 読む練習 六 Reading practice 6

Congratulations! You have worked through the whole of カタ
カナ and you can now put your learning into practice. There
follows a series of activites which use カタカナ words in a range
of contexts which you might encounter if you visit Japan or if you
watch TV programmes or videos about Japan.

練習十 *Activity 10*

We will begin with a coffee-shop menu. These popular places
sell an assortment of drinks and light Western-style meals, which
means the menus are written in カタカナ. Once you can read the
menu, you can order your food!

```
***    ルーナ　コーヒーショップ ***
    ホットコーヒー        500 円
    アイスコーヒー        600 円
    ミルクティー          400 円
    レモンティー          500 円
    コーカコーラ          600 円
    オレンジジュース      400 円
    ミルク                350 円

    *  *  *  *  *  *  *  *  *  *  *  *  *  *  *
```

サンドイッチ/サンド
チーズ　　　　　　600 円
ハム　　　　　　　700 円
ミックス　　　　　700 円

スパゲッティ
ナポリタン　　　　700 円
ミートソース　　　800 円

ピザトースト　　　600 円
サラダ　　　　　　500 円
パフェ　　　　　　700 円
アップルパイ　　　700 円
ケーキ　　　　　　500 ~ 800 円

1 What is the name of this coffee shop? (clue: There is a link with the moon!)
2 What two types of coffee can you buy?
3 What two types of tea can you buy?
4 How much (円 = *yen*) is Coca-Cola?
5 How much does an orange juice cost?
6 What types of sandwich filling can you order?
7 How much would you pay for a meat sauce spaghetti dish?
8 How much would a drink of milk, pizza toast and apple pie cost in total?
9 You have a maximum of 1,000 yen to spend. What drink and main meal would you choose?
10 Which two desserts cost 700 yen?

練習十一 *Activity 11*

Insight

You learned in the introduction to this book and to this unit that カタカナ is used a lot nowadays in advertising. This is because it has the effect of making words stand out (as we use capital letters or italics). Native Japanese words written in カタカナ require a knowledge of Japanese vocabulary to work out their meanings.

In this activity, you should recognize all the words because they are the names of well-known Japanese companies. Different fonts have been chosen for this activity so that you can get used to reading different styles. These styles are used frequently, for example, on neon signs. A checklist of Japanese companies written in *rōmaji* is also given – but not all appear in the activity! So now work out which companies are advertising in the signs.

1 トヨタ
2 ソニー
3 カシオ
4 ナショナル
5 サンヨー
6 ミツビシ

Checklist

Sony, Toyota, Sanyo, National, Mitsubishi, Honda, Casio, Seiko, Yamaha, Nikon, Suzuki, Kawasaki, Matsui, Subaru.

練習十二 *Activity 12*

Electrical stores housing the latest gadgets can be found all over Japan. Most electrical gadgets are given foreign names and so are written in カタカナ. Look at the floor plan, and answer the questions below.

Floor 6	ファン、ヒーター、エアコン、トイレ
Floor 5	テレビ、DVD、ビデオ、レーザーディスク
Floor 4	ファックス、ワープロ、トイレ
Floor 3	コンピューター、プリンター、ソフト
Floor 2	カメラ、ディジカメ、レンズ、フィルム、トイレ
Floor 1	CDプレーヤ、ステレオ、アイポッド、MP3プレーヤ
Basement	ディジタル・ラジオ、コンピュータ・ゲーム

1 On which floors are the toilets?
2 Which floor do you think specializes in computer equipment?
3 Besides computers, what else is sold on this floor?
4 Which floor sells air conditioners?
5 What is being sold on the fifth floor?
6 Where can you buy a camera lens?
7 Where can you buy computer games?
8 How many floors sell audio equipment?
9 As well as word processors, what else can you buy on the fourth floor?
10 Which floor would you go to for an iPod?

Insight

You will sometimes find alternative katakana spellings, especially where the pronunciation of the word may not be clear, for example people's names. Another example is computer, which you will find spelled both with a line at the end and without – either is acceptable:

コンピューター or コンピュータ

練習十三 *Activity 13*

Match the currencies in the left column with the countries in the right (some may require a little guesswork!).

1	ポンド	a	フィリピン
2	ペソ	b	アメリカ
3	ユーロ	c	イギリス
4	ドル	d	スイス
5	フラン	e	インド
6	ルピー	f	イタリア

練習十四 *Activity 14*

There follows a list of world currency rates from a Japanese newspaper. Can you work out the countries and currencies listed? Use your answers from Activity 13 to get you started on this task. The country is given first, followed immediately by the currency with no gap.

Insight

You will notice that three 漢字 are included in the list, these are 米 (see Unit 6, Section 6.2), 英 (this is the 漢字 for England) and 南 (see Unit 8, Section 8.9). This is because many countries can be written using a 漢字 name as well as being phonetically written in katakana.

米ドル	134.65円
ユーロ	117.36
英ポンド	192.77
スイスフラン	79.65
カナダドル	84.79
メキシコペソ	15.76
オーストラリアドル	69.99
ニュージーランドドル	57.69
南アフリカランド	13.19
サウジアラビアリアル	36.49
インドルピー	2.94
タイバーツ	3.13
シンガポールドル	73.82
マレーシアリンギ	–
インドネシアルピア	1.43
フィリピンペソ	2.78

練習十五 *Activity 15*

Finally, here is a set of カタカナ signs from photographs taken in Tokyo. Can you read them and work out the English meaning? がんばって (*ganbatte*) – good luck!

1

Which famous restaurant is this?

2

カラオケ館

What activity can you do here?

3

オープニングセール

What is happening at this shop?

4

ビデオ
と
本

5

リサイクル
と環境

The two *kanji* mean **environment**. What are people being asked to do?

6

カレーハウス CoCo

What is CoCo?

7

バレンタインDAY

8

ビール

9

デザート

10

Eメール

11

新品台数限定品

12

トヨタ

13 シングルモルト

14 ワイン

15 クリスマスツリー

What type of tree is this?

What type of whisky is this?

16

ニコラス・ケイジ　メグ・ライアン

大ヒット
上映中！

京都松竹座

ゴーストを超える感動に全米が泣いた！

かつて地上に存在したことのない、ピュアな恋。

シティ・オブ・エンジェル

What is the title of the film? (bottom line)
What are the actors' names? (above picture)

9.11 書く練習 七 Writing practice 7

This short activity is designed to help you write your name in カタカナ. A short list of popular first names follows. Try saying your name out loud and matching the appropriate カタカナ symbol to each syllable. You will need to refer back to the various rules given in this unit. For example, the name **Laura** has the sounds *lō ra*. The nearest to these sounds are:

ローラ (*rōra*)

And **Christopher** sounds out as *k ri s to phaa*. In Japanese, this becomes:

クリストファー (*kurisutofā*)

If you know a Japanese person, work out your name and get them to check it. Here is a list of 20 names to help you.

Anna	アナ	(*ana*)
Cathy	カシー	(*kashiī*)
Clare	クレア	(*kurea*)
Diana	ダイアナ	(*daiana*)
Hilary	ヒラリー	(*hirariī*)
Jane	ジェイン	(*jein*)
Mary	メアリー	(*meariī*)
Michelle	ミシェル	(*misheru*)
Sara	セーラ	(*seēra*)
Sue	スー	(*suū*)
Andrew	アンドリュー	(*andoryū*)
Bill	ビル	(*biru*)
Brad	ブラッド	(*buraddo*)
Greg	グレッグ	(*gureggu*)
John	ジョン	(*jon*)
Mike	マイク	(*maiku*)
Paul	ポール	(*po-ru*)
Robert	ロバート	(*roba-to*)

| Steve | スティーブ | (sutiību) |
| Tom | トム | (tomu) |

9.12 終りに Conclusion

You have covered the whole of the カタカナ syllabary
in this unit, including the various rules and adaptations of
non-Japanese words. You have had opportunities to read a wide
range of words and to identify typical street signs. Hopefully
you have discovered that, because カタカナ is used to write
non-Japanese (and often English words), it can be fun and very
accessible. There is a lot to take in, so treat this unit as one
you can keep re-visiting and that you can enjoy! And look for
opportunities to read カタカナ around you (TV programmes,
newspapers, magazines, visits to Japan) so that you can impress
your friends and family!

9.13 Five things to remember

Five important things to remember from Unit 9:

- *Katakana* symbols represent the same sounds as hiragana
  symbols and there are the same number – it is the symbols
  themselves that are different.
- There are four main uses for *katakana*: words borrowed from
  other languages; non-Japanese names; making words stand out
  in advertising; plant and animal classification.
- *Katakana* symbols are angular in shape, whereas *hiragana*
  symbols are more rounded.
- If you are planning a visit to Japan, you will find it very useful
  to be able to read *katakana*, especially when reading menus.
- Reading *katakana* is like cracking a code – once you can sound
  out the symbols, you can usually relate the word to an English
  meaning, and this gives a great feeling of achievement!

10

第十課
Unit 10

In this unit, you will:

- *learn to read different types of text including:*
  - *cooking instructions*
  - *cartoons*
  - *weather forecast*
  - *song lyrics*
  - *haiku (short poems)*
- *learn the basics for reading and writing letters*

10.1 はじめに Introduction

The aim of this unit is to pull together everything you have learned throughout this book and apply it to reading Japanese texts. There are many types of text which use different styles of writing and have different levels of difficulty. This unit will get you started on reading and will introduce you to some techniques for accessing text which you can then build on.

Pre-activities

Some tips on grammar functions and particles are given first, and you can refer back to these as necessary. Where 漢字 which have been introduced in earlier units appear in a text, there is a short pre-activity for you to see how many you can remember. However, do not worry if you cannot remember them all, the activity is simply a device to get you thinking about what you have learned and for making connections. Check the answers to these pre-activities in the back before proceeding and, if you want to look back to where the 漢字 was first introduced, remember that you can look up the English meaning in the index, and this will refer you back to that unit.

Main activities

You will be asked to mark parts of the texts as a way of identifying and separating different words and features. This is especially helpful, because Japanese writing does not normally have gaps between words (as you will notice in the texts that follow).

Insight

You could use different-coloured highlighter pens or use different types of markings (e.g. circle, underline, overline). Or you could copy the relevant parts of the text onto paper and mark them.

10.2 Grammar functions

Read through the information that follows, but do not worry if you are not clear about all of it, because the texts will have practical examples, and you can then refer back to the summaries beneath the text to consolidate your learning.

Sentence order (1)

Every noun in a Japanese sentence is usually followed by a particle. A particle is a grammar marker which tells you the function of the noun it marks. Let us look at some examples to help you understand this. In English, the sentence order tells you the function of the main sentence parts:

I ate Japanese food.
- *I* is the **subject** of the sentence (who ate) and comes at the beginning of the sentence.
- *ate* is the **verb**.
- *Japanese food* is the **object** of the sentence (what I ate) and comes after the verb.

This order is called SVO (subject, verb, object). We also use particle-type words (called **prepositions**) such as *with*, *by* and *at*:
*I ate Japanese food **at** home **with** chopsticks.*
The word *at* marks *home* and *with* marks *chopsticks*. They are placed before (**pre**-position) the noun they mark.

Sentence order (2)

This is what happens in Japanese:

私は　和食を　食べました　　*I Japanese cuisine ate*
- 私 (I) is followed by the particle は. It marks the **subject** of the sentence.
- 和食 (Japanese food) is followed by the particle を. It marks the **object** of the sentence.

The order in Japanese is SOV (subject, object, verb).

There are other particles with different functions, such as で (*with*):

私は　はしで　和食を　食べました　*I chopsticks with Japanese food ate*

However, the order of the Japanese sentence is more flexible than the English order because the particles, not the order, tell you the functions of the different parts. So you could say:

私は 和食を はしで 食べました *I Japanese food*
chopsticks with ate

But the verb **always** comes at the end of the sentence.

Particles

Particles are always placed **after** the noun or time expression they mark. Look at the diagram showing the key particles.

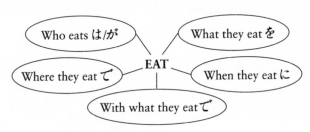

Here is a list of common particles:

は (pronounced *wa* as a particle, not *ha*) topic or subject marker of sentence

が (*ga*) subject marker of verb

を (*o*) object marker of sentence

で (*de*)   **1** with, by: はしで (**with chopsticks**); 電車で (**by train**)

       2 place where action happens: レストランで (**at/in the restaurant**)

に (*ni*)   **1** to (direction): 東京に (**to Tokyo**) (also can use へ pronounced *e*)

       2 at, on (after time): 月曜日に (**on Monday**); 一時に (**at one o'clock**)

       3 at, in, on (place/position): 東京に住んでいます (**I live in Tokyo**)

の (*no*) **1** of, 's: 日本の米 (**Japan's rice** or **Japanese rice**)

2 links a noun with its position: 山の上 (**mountain's top** or **on top of the mountain**)

と (*to*) **1** and (between nouns): 日本と米国 (**Japan and America**)

2 with (accompanied by): 日本人と (**with a Japanese person**)

Insight
Quick translation tips

You will be given lots of pointers throughout this unit, so this is a summary list for you to refer back to as necessary.

1 Find the topic/subject of the sentence by looking for は:

私は 本を 読みます (I book read); subject is 私 (I)

2 Then translate 'backwards' from the end of the sentence:

（私 は）　本を　読みます

book　　　read

3 Describing words are generally placed in the same order as English:

私は　古い本を　読みました (I old book read)

Insight
- In the texts that follow, both literal (lit.) and natural English are given to help you understand the phrases and structuring.

- Where relevant or helpful, the meaning of the 漢字 radical is given in brackets. Assume it is a left-hand radical unless stated otherwise.

練習一 *Activity 1* 漫画 *(Manga)*

京都精華大
大学院風刺専攻　　小川　信子

「たしかに『もっと本を読みなさい』
とは言ったけど…」

Insight

漫画 (manga – cartoon) and アニメ (anime – animation)
are very popular in Japan and are known around the
world. Cartoon books fill bookshops and kiosk shelves,
and Japanese people of all ages can be seen reading them on
trains, in bookshops and at home. The one-frame cartoon
here is taken from the Kyoto News, a Japanese newspaper.

It is from the education section and is a joke about 教育ママ
(kyōiku mama) or 'education mothers' who go to great
lengths to ensure their children study hard and get into the
best schools.

Work through this series of activities starting with a review.

1 漢字復習 *Kanji* review

There are three 漢字 in the cartoon and you have learned them all! Do you remember them? They are:

a 本   **b** 読   **c** 言

2 Find and mark these ひらがな words.

a たしかに (*tashika ni*) certainly, indeed
b もっと (*motto*) more
c けど (*kedo*) but

3 Mark these particles and grammar functions.

a を (*o*) object marker
b ...なさい (*nasai*) verb ending indicating a command, in this case read!
c ...とは (*to wa*) used in reported speech (**I said that ...**). は adds emphasis (**I did say ...**)
d 「 indicates open quote mark (close quote mark is 」). 『』 means quote within a quote.

4 翻訳 *Honyaku*   Translation

「たしかに ... とは言った   '*Indeed I did say ...*
『もっと本を読みなさい』   "*Read more books!*"
けど...   *but ...*'

The **but** trails off, the reader fills in the rest from the picture (... **but this is ridiculous!**).

Notice the technique of translating the information outside the double quotes first then adding the part in double quotes. This would be the order in which we would say it in English, whereas in Japanese the I said part comes at the end. Emphasis on たしかに (indeed) is achieved by placing it at the beginning.

練習二 *Activity 2 Cookery instructions*

イラスト　まつもと　きなこ

The sequence is from the children's educational section of a newspaper. There are two sets of simple cooking instructions.

1 漢字復習 *Kanji* review

Write down the English meanings of these 漢字 and カタカナ words:

a 水 (*mizu*)　**b** 玉 (*tama*)　**c** 火 (*hi*)　　**d** 指 (*yubi*)
e テスト　　**f** ティシュ　**g** フライパン

Now mark them in the text. Remember to check your answers in the back before proceeding.

2 Title: 卵をわる (top three pictures)

a Find and mark these 漢字.

卵 (*tamago*) egg 角 (*kado*) corner, edge 当て (*ate*) hit
親指 (*oya yubi*) thumb (*lit.*: parent finger)

b Find and mark these ひらがな words.

わる (*waru*) break   かたい (*katai*) hard
われめ (*wareme*) a crack   あてて (*atete*) put
まえ (= 前 *mae*) front   うしろ (=後ろ *ushiro*) back
ねじる (*nejiru*) twist

c Find and mark these カタカナ words.

コンコン (*konkon*) tap tap (sound)
ポトン (*poton*) with a plop (sound)

d Mark these particles. Remember that particles are positioned after the word they mark.

を   (*o*) positioned after the object of the sentence – the
         object marker (appears two times)
に   (*ni*) to, in, on (appears three times)
と   (*to*) with (placed after the word); and (placed between
         two nouns)

e 翻訳 *Honyaku*   Translation

Title 卵をわる   Breaking an egg
かたい角に   on a hard edge
コンコンと当て   hit with a tap tap
われめに   in the crack
親指をあてて   put (your) thumb
まえとうしろにねじる   twist to the front and back
                                (forwards and backwards)

3 Title: 水玉テスト (lower three pictures – excluding thought bubble)

a Find and mark these 漢字.

油 (*abura*) oil
水玉 (*mizutama*) water ball/drop
指先 (*yubisaki*) fingertip
置き (*oki*) place
落とす (*otosu*) drop
十分 (*jūbun*) enough

b Find and mark these ひらがな and カタカナ words.

たたんだもの (*tatanda mono*) folded (thing)
のばす (*nobasu*) spread
つけて (*tsukete*) switch on, apply (appears twice)
あたためる (温める = *atatameru*) warm up (also appears as あたたまている)
ころがったら (*korogattara*) if (it) rolls
しるし (*shirushi*) sign
じゅっ (*ju*) ping
コンロ (*konro*) hob

c Mark these particles and grammar functions.

を (*o*) object marker (appears five times)
で (*de*) with, by means of
に (*ni*) on, into (three times)
て (*te*) verb ending meaning and
が (*ga*) subject marker
たら (*tara*) verb ending meaning if, when

d 翻訳 *Honyaku*   Translation

Title 水玉テスト	Water-drop test
ティシュをたたんだもので	with a folded tissue
油をのばす	spread the oil
フライパンをコンロに置き	place the frying pan on the hob

火をつけてあたためる	switch on the heat (fire) and warm up
指先に水をつけて	apply water to the fingertip and
フライパンに落とす	drop into the frying pan
水玉がころがったら	if (when) the water drop rolls
十分あたたまってい	(it's) a sign that it is
るしるし	warmed up enough

練習三 *Activity 3 How to make green tea*

The sequence of four instructions on the tea packet on the next page show you how to make perfect Japanese green tea. Once you can read them, you can try making green tea for yourself!

漢字復習 *Kanji* review

Write down the English meanings of these 漢字 words. Then mark them in the text and write down how many times each appears.

| a 飲 | b 人 | c 目 | d 入 | e お茶 |
| f 便 | g 大 | h 出 | i 時 | |

Insight

Here are some general words used throughout the text which are useful to look at first. They will be referred to again in the translations, so use this list as a reference list.

- ~分 (- bun) means share, part, per. 3人分 means three people's worth or three helpings (food).

- ~目 (- me) means -th, -rd, -nd as in 4つ目 (fourth). 1煎目 means first infusion

- *分 (fun) also means minute. 2分 means two minutes.

The vocabulary and translation are now introduced section by section. Once introduced, vocabulary is not repeated in later sections, so you will need to refer back as necessary.

おいしい飲み方

人数分の湯呑みにお湯を
8分目ほど入れてさまします。
お湯の温度約80℃

　湯呑みを湯ざましの代りに
　使用すると便利です。

お茶の葉を急須に入れます。
3人分で6〜8g
（大さじ約1.5杯分）

湯呑みのお湯を急須にあけて、茶葉に
お湯が浸透するのを待ちます。
浸出時間約1分
（濃いお茶が好きな人は
長めに）

※2煎目の浸出時間は約10秒
　（1煎目より熱いお湯を使用）

お茶を注ぐ分量は均等に、
お茶は最後の
一滴まで絞りきりましょう。

Picture 1

a Find and mark these 漢字.

飲み方 (*nomikata*) how to drink
人数 (*ninzū*) number of people
分 (*bun*) part, per 湯 (*yu*) hot water
湯呑み (alternative: 湯飲み = *yu nomi*) teacup
~分目 (*bunme*) parts 温度 (*ondo*) temperature
約 (*yaku*) approximately
湯ざまし (*yuzamashi*) hot water cooler
代りに (*kawari*) in place of, instead of
使用する (*shiyō suru*) use
便利 (*benri*) convenient, handy

b Find and mark these ひらがな words.

おいしい (*oishii*) delicious ほど (*hodo*) about
入れてさまします (*irete samashimasu*) put in and cool

c Mark these particles and grammar functions.

の (*no*) between two nouns indicates that the second noun
   belongs to the first (3)
に (*ni*) **into, in** (2)
お (*o*) before a noun makes the word sound more honorific.
   お湯 (2)
を (*o*) object marker (2)
と (*to*) **if** (1)

d 翻約 *Honyaku*   Translation

Match the Japanese on the left (1–7) with the translation on the
right (i–vii). The first is done for you.

1 おいしい飲み方 (title)   **i** If you use teacups . . . ( )
2 人数分の湯呑みに   **ii** it is handy ( )
3 お湯を8分目ほど入   **iii** instead of a water cooler ( )
   れてさまします。

4 お湯の温度約80度　　**iv** the temperature of the hot water is about 80°C ( )

5 湯呑みを…使用すると　**v** a delicious drinking method (1)

6 湯ざましの代りに　　　**vi** put in about eight parts hot water and cool ( )

7 便利です　　　　　　　**vii** into drinking cups per number of people ( )

Picture 2

a Find and mark these 漢字.

葉 (*ha*) leaves　急須 (*kyūsu*) teapot
3人分 (*sanninbun*) 3 helpings
大さじ (*ōsaji*) tablespoon　約 (see Picture 1))
杯分 (*haibun*) cupful/spoonful

b Circle the particle で (*de*) meaning **for**; の; を; に

c 翻訳　*Honyaku*　　　　Translation
お茶の葉を急須に入　Put the tea leaves in the teapot.
れます。
3人分で6-8g　　　　for three helpings (people) (it is) 6–8 grams

(大さじ約1・5杯分)　(in tablespoons (it's) approximately 1.5 spoonfuls)

Picture 3

a Find and mark these 漢字.

浸透する (*shintō suru*) brew, permeate
待ちます (*machimasu*) wait
侵出 (*shinshutsu*) brewing
時間 (*jikan*) time　1分 (*ippun*) 1 minute
濃い (*koi*) strong, dark

好きな人 (*sukina hito*) people who like
長めに (*nagame ni*) lengthen
1煎目 (*ichimaeme*) the first infusion
10秒 (*jūbyō*) 10 seconds　熱い (atsui) hot

b Mark these particles and grammar functions.

お (honorific) 4; の 3; に 3; を 3; が 2; は 2
より (*yori*) than (placed after)

c 翻訳　*Honyaku*　　　　　　Translation

Match the Japanese on the left (1–7) with the correct translation on the right (i–vii).

1	湯呑みのお湯を	**i**	the hot water on the tea leaves ( )
2	急須にあけて	**ii**	lengthen (the time) ( )
3	茶葉にお湯が	**iii**	put in the teapot ( )
4	浸透するのを待ちます	**iv**	wait for it (the hot water . . .) to brew ( )
5	浸出時間約1分	**v**	people who like strong tea ( )
6	濃いお茶が好きな人は	**vi**	the hot water in the teacups ( )
7	長めに	**vii**	brewing time (is) about 1 minute ( )

Asterisked part: *The brewing time for the second infusion (refill) is about ten seconds.*

2nd bracketed part: *Use hot water that is hotter than for the first infusion.*

Picture 4

a Find and mark these 漢字.

注ぐ (*sosogu*) pour into　分量 (*bunryō*) quantity
均等に (*kintō ni*) uniformly　最後 (*saigo*) final
一滴 (*itteki*) one drop　絞り (*shibori*) squeeze, extract

b Grammar points

まで (*made*) up to
~きりましょう (*kirimashō*) let's finish . . .

c 翻訳 *Honyaku*   Translation

お茶を注ぐ分量は均等に   pour the quantity of tea
                                                        uniformly
お茶は . . . 絞りきりましよう   (let's) squeeze out the tea
最後の一滴まで   to the final drop

練習四 *Activity 4*

天気予報 (Tenki yohō) *The weather forecast*

The weather forecast shown on the next page is taken from a
Kyoto newspaper. Its title (top left-hand corner) is:

きょうの天気 (*kyō no tenki*) Today's weather

1 漢字復習 *Kanji* review

Decode the place names that follow (refer to map of Japan in
Unit 8, Section 8.9).

a 大阪   **b** 東京   **c** 札幌   **d** 京都

Now find them on the weather report (look at the left side of the
text) and mark them (京都 appears four times).

Insight

You might find it helpful to copy and enlarge the map.
This will help when you are marking and underlining it
and will also leave you with a mark-free original that you
can read later to see how well you have remembered all the
information.

28日21時「ひまわり5号」撮影

28日21時

（京都・彦根地方、舞鶴海洋気象台調べ）

あすの天気

29日は弱い気圧の谷の影響で、朝のうち雲が多いだろう。その後は高気圧におおわれてだいたい晴れの天気になる見込み。日中の気温は24度ぐらいまで上がり、前日と同じぐらいの暖かさになりそう。

2 Key

Below the written text (beginning 29 日 . . .) there is a key consisting of two boxes. Can you see them?

The box with the straight line in the middle indicates のち (*nochi*) which means later. For example: means **sunny later cloudy**.

The box with the slanting line indicates 時々/一時 (*tokodoki ichiji*) meaning sometimes/for a time. For example: means **sometimes sunny, for a time cloudy**.

3 Look at the left-hand column (きょうの天気).

a Find these place names.

福井 Fukui　福岡 Fukuoka　神戸 Kobe　奈良 Nara
名古屋 Nagoya　鹿児島 Kagoshima

Now answer these questions from the information given in the left-hand column.

b What is the weather going to be like in these places?

　i Tokyo　　**ii** Osaka　　**iii** Fukui　　**iv** Kagoshima

c Name two other cities where it will be:

　i cloudy then sunny.　　　　**ii** sunny then cloudy.

4 Middle and lower picture-symbol columns

a 漢字復習 (*Kanji* review) Write down the meanings of these 漢字.

漢字 iii–vii also represent the days of the week. Which days do they represent? (see Unit 1, Section 1.4). Check your answers in the back, then find them in the text.

i 北	ii 南	iii 金	iv 土
v 月	vi 火	vii 水	

> **Insight**
>
> You should have identified 京都 (Kyoto) four times in these
> columns. The other place name (also mentioned four times) is
> 滋賀 (Shiga). After both these place names are these 漢字:
> 北部 (hokubu) and 南部 (nanbu). 部 means **part**, therefore
> **north part** and **south part** (of the Kyoto and Shiga areas).
> The middle column is today's weather, the lower column is
> the forecast for the 30th–4th.

Now answer these questions.

b What is today's weather like in:

   i the north part of Kyoto (area)
   ii the south part of Shiga (area)
   iii the south part of Kyoto (area)?

c What is the weather forecast for:

   i south Kyoto on Friday
   ii south Kyoto on Tuesday
   iii north Kyoto on Sunday
   iv north Shiga on Saturday
   v south Shiga on Wednesday
   vi north Kyoto on Monday?

d On which day and where might you need an umbrella?
(Two answers)

5 Right-side pictures (top and bottom)

a 日 preceded by a number indicates a date.
3日 means *3rd* (day).
時 preceded by a number indicates o'clock.

3時 means *3 o'clock*.
Look at the top satellite picture. When was it taken? (time and date)

b The lower picture has a number of circular symbols to the right followed by 漢字. You learned most of these in Units 6 and 7. Can you identify them now? They are quite small, the size of a real newspaper:

   i 晴   **ii** 曇 (also look up 雲)
iii 雨   **iv** 雷   **v** 雪

Look back to the previous units if you need to, then check your answers in the back and mark the terms in the text (some are quite small).

c There are four other circular symbols with weather terms. Find and mark them:

快晴 good weather 霧 mist, fog
風向・力 wind direction/strength   みぞれ sleet

6 The text

A short text is located above the picture–symbol columns. Go through steps i–iv that follow, then try your own translation before looking at step v (the translation).

  i Find and highlight the following 漢字 words and phrases. What do they mean?

    a 29日   **b** 雲   **c** 高
    d 晴れ   **e** 天気   **f** 上

  ii Find and highlight the following 漢字 words and phrases:

    a 弱い (*yowai*) weak
    b 気圧 (*kiatsu*) atmospheric pressure
    c 谷 (*tani*) valley (trough)

d 影響 (*eikyō*) influence, effect

e 朝 (*asa*) morning

f 多い (*ooi*) many

g その後 (*sono go*) after that

h 高気圧 (*kōkiatsu*) high pressure

i 見込み (*mikomi*) expectation

j 日中 (*nitchū*) all day

k 気温 (*kion*) temperature

l 度 (*do*) degrees

m 上がり (*agari*) to rise

n 前日 (*zenjitsu*) previous day

o 同じ (*onaji*) same

p 暖かさ (*atatakasa*) warmth

iii Find and mark these ひらがな words:

a うち (*uchi*) during

b だろう (*darō*) will probably

c ...におおわれて (*ni oowarete*) be covered by (literal translation)

d だいたい (*daitai*) generally

e ...になる (*ni naru*) become ...

f ぐらい (*gurai*) about (+2)

g まで (*made*) up to

h ...になりそう (*ni narisō*) it looks like it will be(come) ...(そう = seem, look like)

iv Find and mark these particles and grammar functions:

は (*wa*) topic marker (3)   の (*no*) of, 's (7)

で (*de*) through, by means of (+1)

が (*ga*) subject marker (1)   と (*to*) as (1)

Insight

ヒント Try to translate the text yourself before working through step v. Remember: find the topic or subject, then work through the sentence/phrase from the end.

29日は 弱い気圧の谷の影響で	The 29th (start from the end of this sentence and work backwards): through the influence (because of the effect) of a trough of low (weak) pressure
朝のうち 雲が多いだろう	during the morning the clouds will probably be many (there will be a lot of cloud)
その後は . . . 見込み	after that . . . it is expected (that)
高気圧におおわれて	high pressure will spread and
だいたい晴れの天気になる	generally it will be (come) fine weather
日中の気温は 24度ぐらいまで上がり	the daytime temperature will rise up to about 24 degrees
. . . になりそう 前日と同じぐらいの暖かさ	it looks like it will be about the same warmth as the previous day (yesterday)

練習五 *Activity 5*

手紙 (Tegami) *Letters*

This section will first get you to read a letter which is handwritten, then give you some tips for writing a letter yourself!

This letter is written downwards; you start reading at the top right, down the column. This is the traditional way of writing letters, but many Japanese people nowadays write in Western style, horizontally from left to right. Writing downwards can give a letter a more formal or traditional tone. This is a New Year's greetings card, and as this is a traditional custom, such cards are often (but not always) written in the traditional downwards style.

新年
明けまして　おめでとう　ございます
お手紙　ありがとう　ございました。　夫と　うれしく
読ませて　いただきました。　昨年は　日本で
ヘレンに　お目にかかれて　うれしかった　です。
その時の写真を　送ります。　来年の　夏は
イギリスに　行きたいと　思っています。
又、お会いできることを　楽しみに。
それでは　お元気で、
一九九九年　元旦

山本　花子

1 Start by identifying and marking 漢字 you have already been introduced to. As before, see how many you can remember, then check the answers in the back before proceeding further.

a 新年 **b** 明 **c** 手 **d** 読 **e** 昨 **f** 日本
g 目 **h** 時 **i** 行 **j** 思 **k** 会 **l** 楽
m 気 **n** 年 **o** 旦 **p** 山本 **q** 子

2 Find and mark these set phrases and read the explanations.

a お目にかかれて (*o-me ni kakarete*) lit. 'I was able to set eyes on you'. This is a respectful way of saying 'I was able to see/meet you'.
b ...楽しみに (*tanoshimi ni*) I am looking forward to ... This phrase ends with に. The full sentence would end with しています (*shiteimasu*), but this is often omitted.
c お元気で (*o-genki de*) Take care!

3 Now mark these 漢字 words and phrases.

a 明けまして (*akemashite*) to dawn (from 明ける (*akeru*))
b お手紙 (*o-tegami*) letter
c 夫 (*otto*) husband
d 昨年 (*sakunen*) last year
e 写真 (*shashin*) photograph
f 送ります (*okurimasu*) send
g 来年 (*rainen*) next year
h 夏 (*natsu*) summer
i 又 (*mata*) again

j 元旦 (*gantan*) New Year's Day

k 花子 Hanako (girl's name; 花 means 'flower')

4 Next mark these ひらがな words and phrases.

a おめでとうございます (*omedetō gozaimasu*)
congratulations

b ありがとうございました (*arigatō gozaimashita*) thank
you (for what you have done)

c うれしく (*ureshiku*) happily うれしかった (*ureshikatta*)
was/were happy

d いただきました (*itadakimashita*) received (see 6c in this
section)

e できる (*dekiru*) be able to

f それでは (*sore dewa*) and so, well, finally (used at end
of letter)

5 Mark these two カタカナ words.

a ヘレン (*Heren*) Helen   **b** イギリス (*Igirisu*) England

6 Find and mark these particles and grammar functions.

a お (*o*) adds tone of respect to nouns (put before the word)
(2; also see 2a and 2c above).

b と (*to*) and, with (see also 6k).

c 読ませて (*yomasete*) (you) let me read + いただきま
した (I received), *lit.* 'I received you letting me read'. It is a
polite way of acknowledging something which someone has
done for you. Another example is: 休ませていただきま
した (*yasumasete itadakimashita*) (**You) let me take a break.**

d は (*wa*) topic marker (2).

e で (*de*) in, at (particle used to mark the place where
something happens).

f に (*ni*) with, to (2; also see 2a this section).

g その (*sono*) that.

h の (*no*) see notes at beginning of unit (2).

i を (*o*) object marker (2).

j 行きたい (*ikitai*) I want to go (たい = want to).

k と思っています (*. . . to omotteimasu*) I think that . . .
(と here means that).

l こと (*koto*) placed after a verb this can be translated as
. . . **ing**. Therefore: できること (*dekiru koto*) **being able to**.

7 翻訳 *Honyaku* Translation

This time, you are going to do some of the work! The translation
follows, phrase by phrase. However, it is not in order, and your
task is to work out the correct order. Some of it may be obvious
from the English (!), but keep referring back to the text and points
(1–6) of this section so that you get a good understanding of how
the letter is structured.

a *lit.* 'Next year's summer I think that I want to go to England'
= Next summer I hope to . . . /would like to . . .

b With my husband (my husband and I) read your letter happily
(with pleasure).

c I look forward to being able to meet again.

d Thank you for your letter.

e I am sending (you) the photographs of (/from) that time.

f Well, take care.

g *lit.* 'the new year has dawned, congratulations' =
Happy New Year!

h New Year's Day, 1999. (From) Hanako Yamamoto (in
Japanese, the surname precedes the first name).

i I was happy that last year I was able to meet with Helen in
Japan. (The Japanese often use your name instead of saying
you.)

10.3 書く練習 Writing letters

1 Let's start by looking at some of the features of the letter you
have just read.

a Did you notice that the date is written at the end of the letter, and is followed by the name of the writer? This is standard practice.

b Hanako (the writer) begins with a greeting, in this case **Happy New Year**. You will learn some more seasonal greetings in the next section.

c Hanako then says thank you for the letter she received. You can use this structure to thank someone for something they have sent you such as:

プレゼント **present**; はがき **postcard**; カード **card**

Just add ありがとうございました **(thank you)** after the item.

d Hanako brings the letter to a close with それでは、お元気で **(Well, take care)**.

2 Now let us look at useful phrases and techniques you can use to write a letter to a Japanese friend.

a Begin with their name followed by さん *(san)* if you know the person well or さま *(sama)* for a very formal letter. In this case, you might use the surname. For example:

花子さん *(Hanako san)*

山本さま *(Yamamoto-sama)* (or 花子さま *Hanako-sama*)

b Rather than beginning with an enquiry about a person's health (**How are you?**), the Japanese tend to comment on the weather first and then maybe a comment about the person's health. Here are some useful phrases for different times of the year:

良いお年を *(yoi o-toshi o)* Have a good year (normally used before New Year's day).

明けましておめでとう *(akemashite omodetō)* Happy New Year (used during New Year).

メリークリスマス *(merī kurisumasu)* Merry Christmas.

まだまだ寒さが続いています (*mada mada samusa ga tsuzuiteimasu*) The cold weather continues.

ようやく春がきました (*yōyaku haru ga kimashita*) At last spring has come.

きびしい暑さが続いています (*kibishii atsusa ga tsuzuiteimasu*) The unrelenting heat continues.

静かに秋がやってきています (*shizuka ni aki ga yatte kiteimasu*) Autumn has crept up on us quietly.

c Enquiries about health: お元気ですか (*o-genki desu ka*) How are you? (informal) お元気でお過しでしようか (*o-genki de o-sugoshi deshō ka*) How are you? (formal)

d Closing phrases:

Either: それでは、お元気で (see 1d in this section) Well, take care.

Or: では、お体に気をつけて (*dewa, o-karada ni ki o tsukete*) Well, take care of yourself.

お返事お待ちしています (*o-henji o-machi shiteimasu*) I wait for your reply.

さようなら (*sayōnara*) Goodbye.

かしこ (*kashiko*) sincerely (used by women; formal).

e You don't need to use an equivalent of **Dear** or **from** when writing a letter. The person's name plus さん/さま (see 2a in this section) and your own name at the end (after the date) is enough.

Insight

If you are writing a brief note or postcard, you can miss out the seasonal greetings and closing phrases and use this pair of phrases instead: 前略 (zenryaku) Greetings! (used at the beginning); 早々 (sō sō) Excuse the rush (used at the end).

練習六 Activity 6

さくら (Sakura) *The cherry blossom song*

This is perhaps the most well-known Japanese song. The music is reproduced as well on the following page, so that you can try singing it once you have studied its meaning! Notice that the lyrics are written in ひらがな, so that it is clear which sound fits which note.

Here are the words of the song, this time with 漢字 as well. The rōmaji is written to the side. You could write the rōmaji below the ひらがな on the music, but try instead to read the ひらがな, because this will be very good reading practice! Here is the text:

桜、桜	*Sakura, Sakura*
野山も郷も	*noyama mo sato mo*
見渡す限り	*miwatasu kagiri*
霞か雲か	*kasumi ka kumo ka*
朝日に匂う	*asahi ni niou*
桜、桜	*Sakura, Sakura*
花盛り	*hanazakari*

1 What are the meanings of the following 漢字?

a 山	**b** 見
c 雲	**d** 朝 (Unit 10, Activity 4, 6 ii e)
e 日	**f** 花 (Unit 10, Activity 5, 3 k)

2 Find and mark these 漢字 words.

a 桜 (*sakura*) cherry blossom (×4)
b 野山 (*noyama*) fields and hills
c 郷 (*sato*) home town
d 見渡す (*miwatasu*) survey the scene, look out over
e 限り (*kagiri*) endless, everywhere; as far as

224

さくら

f 霞 (*kasumi*) mist (notice the rain radical)
g 朝日 (*asahi*) morning sun
h 匂う (*niou*) be fragrant
i 花盛り (*hanazakari*) (flowers) in full bloom

3 Find and mark these particles and grammar functions.

a も . . . も (*mo . . . mo*) both . . . and
b か . . . か (*ka . . . ka*) either . . . or
c に (*ni*) in

翻訳 *Honyaku* Translation

This time, you are going to try the translation completely by yourself! Song lyrics and poems often use very minimal language, and use words to evoke a sense of what is being described rather than spelling it all out. When translating into English, there are a number of stages to follow:

i Translate individual words and phrases (here done for you).
ii Put together in 'literal' English.
iii Consider what meanings are being conveyed and change into a more natural English structure.
iv At this stage, translators need to decide whether it is more important to keep closely to the original Japanese or to 'interpret' the text and put their own individual mark on it. This may depend on the text or on the purpose of the translation. Certainly with poems and songs, it may be necessary to change words in order to make the song fit the tune or for the poem to retain its structure, rhythm or rhyme.

Insight

In the case of this song, you will be singing it in Japanese, so focus on conveying the sense of the Japanese words in more natural English (but why not have a go at getting the English to fit the tune, too!). There is a sample translation at the back so that you can check for meaning, but as long as the general meaning is correct, other versions are equally acceptable.

練習七 *Activity 7* 俳句 *Haiku*

Haiku were developed in Japan, but nowadays are known and written all over the world. They are a style of poetic writing using a small number of words to convey a much deeper feeling or emotion. Traditionally, the poems were observations of nature which would evoke a strong sense of the scene described or of the emotions underlying it. Modern haiku explore many themes and continue to be popular both in Japan and internationally.

A haiku is traditionally a 17-syllable poem of three lines: 5–7–5 (five syllables, seven syllables, five syllables). The four great masters of Japanese haiku were Bashō (1644–94), Buson (1716–84), Issa (1762–1826) and Shiki (1867–1902). A few haiku by these great masters follow – you are going to have a go at translating them! A choice of English translations of a word will often be given so that you can 'experiment' with your translation. There are sample translations at the back so that you can check on meanings. Most translators try to capture the sense of the poem in English without retaining the 5–7–5 form, but once you have the meaning, you could try to reduce it to 17 syllables!

Haiku 1

涼しさや	*suzushisa ya*	子規 Shiki
青田の中に	*aota no naka ni*	
一つ松	*hitotsu matsu*	

1 You have met these 漢字 in this book. What do they mean?

   a 青   **b** 田   **c** 中   **d** 一

2 The new 漢字 words are:

   a 涼しさ (*suzushisa*) coolness (*water* radical)
   b 松 (*matsu*) pine tree (*tree* radical)

3 Particles and grammar functions

    a や (*ya*) A poetic convention, for emphasis translated as **the** or **a** (like は *wa*). Some translators use . . . after the word to set the scene. For example: 涼しさや The coolness . . .

    b の (*no*) of   **c** に (*ni*) in

    d 一つ (*hitotsu*) one (item); a single (thing)

Haiku 2

古池や	*furuike ya*	芭蕉	Bashō
蛙飛び込む	*kawazu tobikomu*		
水の音	*mizu no oto*		

1 You have met these 漢字 in this book. What do they mean?

    a 古   **b** 水   **c** 音

2 The new 漢字 words are:

    a 池 (*ike*) pond (water radical)
    b 蛙 (*kawazu*) frog (insect radical)
    c 飛び込む (*tobikomu*) leap/plunge/dive/jump into

3 Particles and grammar functions

    a や (*ya*) see 3a above   **b** の (*no*) of

Haiku 3

夕風や	*yūkaze ya*	蕪村	Buson
水青鷺の	*mizu aosagi no*		
脛を打つ	*hagi o utsu*		

1 You have met these 漢字 in this book. What do they mean?

    a 風 (p. 164, 5c)   **b** 水   **c** 青

2 The new 漢字 words are:

    a 夕 (*yū*) evening
    b 鷺 (*sagi*) heron (bird radical, below)
    c 脛 (*hagi*) leg, shin (flesh radical)
    d 打つ (*utsu*) hit, knock/lap against (*hand* radical)

3 Particles and grammar functions

    a や (*ya*) see Haiku 1, 3a   **b** の (*no*) of
    c を (*o*) object marker

Haiku 4

秋の夜や   *aki no yo ya*   一茶   Issa
旅の男の   *tabi no otoko no*
針仕事   *hari shigoto*

1 You have met these 漢字 in this book. What do they mean?

    a 旅   **b** 男   **c** 針

2 The new 漢字 words are:

    a 秋 (*aki*) autumn   **b** 夜 (*yo*) night
    c 仕事 (*shigoto*) work

3 Particles and grammar functions

    a や (*ya*) see I, 3a   **b** の (*no*) of, connects linked words

10.4 テスト Test yourself

There follows a unit-by-unit selection of *kanji* that you have learned in the main *kanji* units of this book. Can you remember their English meanings?

Unit 1

木　森　林　川　山　金　火　竹　田　石

Unit 2

口　目　女　子　男　人　車　馬　好　門

Unit 3

月　日　七　十　百　円　千　万　年　九

Unit 4

見　聞　読　言　話　語　食　飲　物　出

Unit 6

古　小　大　高　新　黒　白　広　安　青
中　上　下　国　肉　校　母　父　雨　島

Unit 7

時　畑　体　信　泊　針　転　姦　町　村

Unit 8

市　館　公　酒　店　魚　茶　園　住　駅

行　内　外　席　北　南　西　東　右　左

開　閉

10.5 終りに Conclusion

おめでとうございます (*omedetō gozaimasu*)
Congratulations! You have completed *Read and write Japanese script*. I hope that you now feel you have a good grounding in Japanese reading and writing and are ready to take your study further and tackle new challenges! Look for every opportunity to use your learning so that you can consolidate it, and revisit the units in this book to refresh your learning. If you have not yet tackled the spoken language or only have the basics, then how about trying *Get started in Japanese* or *Speak Japanese* next? Also the full *Complete Japanese* course includes unit-by-unit sections on reading to help you build up your reading skill. And please write to me (c/o Hodder) to let me know how you got on with this book.

それでは、さようなら!

Key to the activities

Unit 1

Work it out!

1 c **2** g **3** h **4** i **5** a **6** 1 **7** f **8** j **9** e **10** k
11 b **12** d

Activity 1

a 6 **b** 14 **c** 10 **d** 9 **e** 11 **f** 12 **g** 3 **h** 2 **i** 13 **j** 1
k 7 **l** 4 **m** 8 **n** 5

Activity 2

a 5 **b** 1 **c** 4 **d** 7 **e** 6 **f** 3 **g** 2

Activity 3

1 Wed **2** Tues **3** Sun **4** Fri **5** Sat **6** 1 **7** 1 **8** 2
9 Mon

Unit 2

Work it out!

1 l **2** k **3** g **4** e **5** d **6** a **7** c **8** b **9** h **10** i **11** j
12 f

Activity 1

a 6 **b** 2 **c** 3 **d** 4 **e** 8 **f** 9 **g** 10 **h** 1 **i** 7 **j** 5

Activity 2

1 a Sun **b** Wed **c** Mon **d** Sat
2 4 (4th, 11th, 18th, 25th)
3 Sun

Activity 3

1 April, March
2 a April, July **b** June, Feb, March **c** Sept, Dec
3 a Sun **b** Sat **c** Tues **d** Wed **e** Wed
4 a Mon **b** Wed **c** Sun **d** Mon–Sun **e** Mon

Activity 4

a Sat 14th Feb   **b** Thurs 20th Nov
c Mon 5th May   **d** Sun 10th Sept
e Wed 25th Dec   **f** Fri 1st April

Activity 6

A 1 b **2** c **3** b **4** a **5** c
B 1 a **2** c **3** b **4** a **5** c
C 1 c, ii **2** a, iii **3** c, i **4** b, ii **5** b, i **6** a, iii
   7 b, i **8** c, i **9** a, iii **10** a, ii

Activity 7

1 a Hayashi **b** Morita **c** Moriyama **d** Yamakawa
   e Takeyama **f** Mori **g** Kita **h** Ishikawa
2 a Kaneda **b** Takeda **c** Ishida **d** Yamada
   e Kawada

Test yourself

1 a man **b** wood **c** power **d** gold
2 a population **b** Japan **c** girl **d** gateway
   e volcano **f** men and women
3 a ii **b** vi **c** vii **d** v **e** i **f** iii **g** iv
4 a Yamada **b** Takeyama **c** Morita **d** Mori **e** Ishida
5 Check writing sections/charts.

Unit 3

Introduction

a iii   **b** iv   **c** ii

Activity 1

1 a iv   **b** vi   **c** v   **d** i   **e** ii   **f** iii
3 a 6   **b** 4   **c** 5   **d** 8

Activity 2

3 h, g, b, e, i, c, d, f, a, j

4 a 9   **b** 6   **c** 7   **d** 19   **e** 17   **f** 13   **g** 20   **h** 50   **i** 70   **j** 21
k 32   **l** 43   **m** 54   **n** 65   **o** 76   **p** 87   **q** 88   **r** 99

Activity 3

1 e, f, b, d, c, h, g, a; 600 is missing.
2 a 8,000   **b** 5,000   **c** 7,000   **d** 6,000   **e** 2,000   **f** 1,000
3 a iii   **b** i   **c** iv   **d** ii   **e** v
4 a, e, b, g, d, c, f
    200; 2,000; 2,200; 20,000; 200,000; 2,000,000; 20,000,000
5 a ii   **b** v   **c** vii   **d** vi   **e** iv   **f** i   **g** iii

Activity 4

1 1 b   **2** e   **3** a   **4** d   **5** c
2 1 d   **2** c   **3** f   **4** e   **5** b   **6** a
3 1 11th Nov   **2** 18th Jun   **3** 2nd Oct   **4** 21st Aug
    5 31st Mar   **6** 24th Jun

Activity 5

1 a iv   **b** v   **c** vi   **d** i   **e** iii   **f** ii
2 a iii   **b** v   **c** iv   **d** i   **e** vi   **f** ii

Activity 6

1 a (03) 358–1377   **b** (097) 592–4211
  c (0720) 21–3866   **d** (03) 3593–2704
  e (0279) 221–3154

2 a Sat 5th Dec 1998   **b** Sun 6th Dec 1998
  c Sat 12th Dec 1998
3 Sat 21st Oct 1995

Test yourself

1 45,200 yen (money)
2 Heisei 21 = 2009 (year)
3 03 562 1989 (phone number)
4 March 26th (date)
5 2008 (year)
6 Showa 62 = 1987 (year)

Unit 4

Introduction

1 a mouth **b** ear **c** person **d** eye **e** mountain
  f gate **g** tree **h** sun(day) **i** child
2 a gate and ear **b** eye **c** sun **d** mouth **e** child **f** eye
  g tree **h** mountain

Activity 1

a 4 **b** 2 **c** 7 **d** 6 **e** 5 **f** 1 **g** 3

Activity 2

1 f **2** g **3** e **4** a **5** d **6** b **7** c

Activity 4

1 b **2** e **3** f **4** g **5** a **6** d **7** c

Activity 5

1 e **2** b **3** g **4** f **5** d **6** a **7** c

Activity 6

1 f **2** b **3** c **4** d **5** a **6** e

Activity 7

1 f **2** e **3** b **4** g **5** c **6** a **7** d

Activity 8

1 dealer **2** entrance **3** exit **4** drinking water
5 academic ability **6** buyer **7** holiday **8** Japanese person

Activity 9

1 **1** d **2** e **3** f **4** h **5** k **6** i **7** m **8** b **9** c **10** d
   11 j **12** g **13** l **14** a
2 **a** baibai **b** dokusho **c** nyūgaku **d** shutsunyū **e** inshoku
   f kengaku **g** kyūgaku **h** kenbun

Test yourself

1 **a** horse **b** person **c** woman **d** man **e** child **f** girl
   g boy **h** Japanese person
2 **a** mountain **b** volcano **c** river **d** water **e** fire **f** tree
   g wood **h** forest **i** rice field
3 **a** 1 **b** 5 **c** 60 yen **d** 100 **e** 4,000 yen **f** 20,000
   g gold, money **h** 3,700
4 **a** Sat 11th Sep **b** 20th Aug **c** 1991 (year)
   d Heisei 12th year = Year 2000
5 **a** listen **b** eat **c** drink **d** say **e** talk **f** read **g** sell
   h look **i** buy **j** rest
6 **a** ear **b** mouth **c** foot **d** eye **e** hand

Unit 5

Introduction

1 To write grammar and non-漢字 Japanese words
2 ひらがな
3 Simplified 漢字 with the same pronunciation
4 46

Work it out!

(Reading down): d, f, a, c, b, e

Activity 1

a sushi **b** aki **c** koe **d** tsukue **e** satou/satō **f** seito

Activity 2

7 a 1 **b** 2 **c** 2 **8** け **9** す **15 a** 2 **b** 2 **16** 10 **17** ほ

Activity 3

Set 1 **a** asa **b** te **c** natsu **d** tokei **e** shio **f** nani **g** nuno
Set 2 **a** yoru **b** mimi **c** haru **d** fuyu **e** mura **f** yama
 g mori **h** wan
Set 3 **a** ohayou/ohayō **b** sayounara/ sayōnara **c** neko
 d sensei **e** inu **f** me **g** heso **h** hito **i** rei **j** nihon

Activity 4

a kyaa kyaa   **b** shun shun   **c** shū shū
d chū chū   **e** nyaa nyaa   **f** hyū hyū
g hyoro hyoro   **h** kyoro kyoro

Activity 6

a kyaku **b** kyō **c** gyūnyū **d** shashin
e ja ne **f** chōshoku **g** chūshoku **h** hyaku
i byōin **j** ryokō

Activity 7

a mizu **b** kagi **c** jiten **d** denwa
e tanpopo **f** doki doki **g** gabu gabu

Activity 8

a chotto **b** matte **c** yappari
d gakkō **e** ganbatte **f** massugu

Activity 9

a tabemasu, tabemashita   **b** nomimasu, nomimashita
c mimasu, mimashita   **d** kakimasu, kakimashita
e hanashimasu, hanashimashita

Unit 6

Introduction

a earth **b** tree **c** woman **d** stone
e mouth **f** horse **g** sun **h** moon

Work it out!

a 10 **b** 1 **c** 5 **d** 6 **e** 3 **f** 9 **g** 8 **h** 2 **i** 7 **j** 4

Activity 1

a 6 **b** 9 **c** 4 **d** 10 **e** 8 **f** 3 **g** 1 **h** 5 **i** 2 **j** 7

Activity 2

a 4 **b** 2 **c** 5 **d** 3 **e** 1

Activity 3

a 6 **b** 9 **c** 5 **d** 8 **e** 7 **f** 2 **g** 3 **h** 4 **i** 1

Activity 4

a 4 **b** 1 **c** 5 **d** 3 **e** 7 **f** 2 **g** 8 **h** 6

Activity 5

a 2 **b** 8 **c** 5 **d** 7 **e** 4 **f** 3 **g** 1 **h** 6

Activity 6

a 11 **b** 5 **c** 13 **d** 14 **e** 1 **f** 7 **g** 8 **h** 9 **i** 12 **j** 6
k 3 **l** 4 **m** 15 **n** 17 **o** 2 **p** 10 **q** 16

Activity 8

a takai **b** yasui **c** chiisai **d** ōkii
e sukunai **f** sukoshi **g** furui **h** atarashii
i futoi **j** hiroi **k** shiroi

Test yourself

a 1 above **2** below **3** small
4 big **5** middle (also inside) **6** dog

7 fat	8 a little	9 axe
10 father	11 cow	12 stand
13 old	14 mother	15 wide
16 white	17 rice	18 cheap, safe
19 thread	20 pointed	21 meat
22 hot/bitter	23 rain	24 blue
25 country	26 sound	27 tall, expensive
28 island	29 school	30 black
31 bird	32 snow	33 cloud
34 new	35 thunder	36 electric
37 dove	38 cloudy	39 frost

b 1 Sunday	2 Saturday	3 Wednesday
4 Tuesday	5 start school	6 primary school
7 middle school	8 high school	9 absent from school
10 study visit	11 Japan	12 China
13 America	14 Central America	15 mother country
16 island country	17 beef	18 chicken
19 food	20 drink	21 white rice
22 drinking water	23 train	24 new car
25 secondhand car	26 carriage	27 rickshaw
28 puppy	29 calf	30 swan
31 parents	32 child	33 adult
34 boy	35 girl	36 girl
37 shopping	38 sightseeing	39 entrance
40 exit	41 holiday	

Unit 7

Introduction

1 a wood	b forest	c man	d like
e bright	f listen	g see	h write
i say/words	j sell	k read	l speak
m buy	n rest	o go out	p study
2 a person	b mouth	c earth	d woman
e child	f sun	g moon	h tree
i fire	j rice field	k eye	l say/words
m gold	n car		

Activity 1

a 6 **b** 7 **c** 4 **d** 9 **e** 12 **f** 5 **g** 10 **h** 2 **i** 3 **j** 8
k 11 **l** 1

Activity 4

a	**1** hat radical	**2**	above
b	**1** vegetation	**2**	above
c	**1** lid	**2**	above
d	**1** village	**2**	right side
e	**1** enclosure	**2**	surround
f	**1** yawn	**2**	right side
g	**1** bamboo	**2**	above
h	**1** fire	**2**	below
i	**1** hole	**2**	above
j	**1** cover	**2**	above
k	**1** vapour	**2**	partial surround
l	**1** heart	**2**	below
m	**1** rain	**2**	above

Activity 5

1 i c ii d iii e iv b v a
2 i a ii b iii d iv c
3 i b ii d iii c iv e v f vi a vii g

Test yourself

Row 1: 16, 2, 3, 7
Row 2: 10, 15, 18, 19
Row 3: 9, 20, 17, 5
Row 4: 11, 12, 13, 14
Row 5: 1, 6, 8, 4

Unit 8

Work it out!

a 4 (4) **b** 12 (4) **c** 14 (2) **d** 7 (2) **e** 5 (6) **f** 13 (6) **g** 2 (6)
h 10 (6) **i** 3 (6) **j** 15 (7) **k** 11 (6) **l** 1 (4/6) **m** 9 (4/6)
n 6 (3) **o** 8 (4)

Activity 1

1 h **2** c **3** j **4** k **5** m **6** l **7** b **8** c **9** a **10** d
11 n **12** f **13** o **14** g **15** a **16** i **17** e

Activity 2

1 e **2** f **3** j **4** o **5** n **6** l **7** i **8** a **9** h **10** g **11** k
12 d **13** m **14** b **15** c

Activity 4

1 d **2** b **3** g **4** e **5** f **6** h **7** c **8** a

Activity 5

1 c **2** e **3** b **4** a **5** d

Activity 6

1 toilet	**2** entrance	**3** toilet
4 'Thundergate'	**5** push	**6** pull
7 south gate	**8** north gate	**9** Hiroshima, Osaka
10 grilled (food)	**11** railway station	**12** Fuji Bank
13 opening times	**14** international phone	**15** unreserved
16 unoccupied taxi	**17** Japanese-style room	**18** no admittance
19 no smoking		

Unit 9

Introduction

1 Loan words; foreign names; to make words stand out;
plant/animal classification
2 Part of 漢字
3 46

Work it out!

(in order from top) e, d, a, f, b, c

Activity 1

skirt (**e**) suit (**f**) steak (**c**) cake (**a**) ice (**d**) toast (**b**)

Activity 2

Set 1: 1 g   2 f   3 b   4 c   5 a   6 e   7 d
Set 2: 1 c   2 e   3 d   4 b   5 a
Set 3: 1 f   2 g   3 d   4 a   5 c   6 b   7 h   8 e

Activity 4

1   i d   ii c   iii a   iv e   v b
2   i c   ii e   iii a   iv d   v b
3   i f   ii b   iii e   iv d   v a   vi c   vii g
4   i c   ii e   iii a   iv d   v g   vi b   vii f
5   i g   ii b   iii i   iv e   v j   vi a   vii k   viii h   ix f   x l
    xi c   xii d
6   i a   ii c   iii e   iv d   v f   vi b
7   i b   ii e   iii a   iv c   v d
8   i a   ii c   iii e   iv d   v b

Activity 6

1 h   2 j   3 a   4 c   5 i   6 g   7 b   8 e   9 f   10 d

Activity 7

1 i   2 g   3 j   4 a   5 e   6 d   7 b   8 c   9 f   10 h

Activity 8

1 g   2 b   3 h   4 a   5 l   6 k   7 i   8 e   9 c   10 d
11 f   12 j

Activity 9

1 e viii   2 a ix   3 c v   4 g ii   5 i iii   6 h x   7 d vii
8 j iv   9 f i   10 b vi

Activity 10

1 Luna   2 hot, iced   3 milk, lemon
4 600 yen   5 400 yen   6 cheese, ham, mixed
7 800 yen   8 350 + 600 + 700 = 1,650 yen
9 your choice   10 parfait, apple pie

Activity 11

1 Toyota
2 Sony
3 Casio
4 National
5 Sanyo
6 Mitsubishi

Activity 12

1 Floors 2, 4, 6
2 Floor 3
3 Printers, software
4 Floor 6
5 TV, video, DVD, laserdiscs
6 Floor 2
7 Basement
8 Two: basement, floor 1
9 Fax machines
10 Floor 1

Activity 13

a 2 (Philippines, peso)
b 4 (America, dollar)
c 1 (England, pound (sterling))
d 5 (Switzerland, franc)
e 6 (India, rupee)
f 3 (Italy, euro)

Activity 14

(from top): America dollar, euro, England pound, Swiss franc,
Canada dollar, Mexico peso, Australia dollar, New Zealand dollar,
South Africa rand, Saudi Arabia rial, India rupee, Thai baht,
Singapore dollar, Malaysia ringgit, Indonesia rupiah, Philippine peso

Activity 15

1 McDonald's
2 karaoke
3 opening sale
4 videos and books
5 recycle
6 a curry house
7 Valentine's Day
8 beer
9 dessert
10 e-mail
11 piano
12 Toyota
13 single malt
14 wine
15 Christmas tree
16 City of Angels, Nicholas Cage, Meg Ryan

Unit 10

Activity 1

1 a book **b** read **c** say

Activity 2

1 a water   **b** jewel (ball)   **c** fire   **d** finger
  e test   **f** tissue   **g** frying pan

Activity 3

Kanji review: **a** drink/1   **b** person/3   **c** eye/3   **d** enter/2   **e** tea/5
f convenience/mail/1   **g** big/1   **h** go out/2   **i** time/2
Picture 1:   **d**   **1** v   **2** vii   **3** vi   **4** iv   **5** i   **6** iii   **7** ii
Picture 3:   **c**   **1** vi   **2** iii   **3** i   **4** iv   **5** vii   **6** v   **7** ii

Activity 4

1 a Osaka   **b** Tokyo   **c** Sapporo   **d** Kyoto
3b i cloudy later sunny   **ii** sunny later cloudy
   iii sunny sometimes cloudy   **iv** rainy later cloudy
3c i two of: Nagoya, Fukuoka, Sapporo   **ii** Kobe, Nara
4a i north **ii** south **iii** gold/Friday **iv** earth/Saturday
   v moon/Monday **vi** fire/Tuesday **vii** water/Wednesday
4b i/ii/iii All are cloudy later sunny.
4c i cloudy sometimes sunny   **ii** sunny sometimes cloudy
   iii cloudy sometimes rainy   **iv** cloudy sometimes sunny
   v sunny sometimes cloudy   **vi** cloudy
4d Sunday: North Kyoto and North Shiga
5a 21:00/9 o'clock, 28th
5b i sunny/fine **ii** cloudy (cloud) **iii** rain **iv** thunder **v** snow
6i a 29th **b** cloud **c** tall (high) **d** fine **e** weather **f** above

Activity 5

1 a New Year   **b** bright   **c** hand   **d** read
   e previous   **f** Japan   **g** eye   **h** time
   i go   **j** think   **k** meet   **l** enjoy
   m spirit   **n** year   **o** dawn   **p** Yamamoto
   q child
7 g, d, b, i, e, a, c, f, h

Activity 6

1 a mountain **b** look **c** cloud **d** morning **e** sun
  f flower

Sample translation: Cherry blossom, cherry blossom, over fields and hills, I survey the endless scene (or: as far as the eye can see; or: an endless scene). (like) mist or cloud, fragrant in the morning sun, cherry blossom, cherry blossom, in full bloom.

Activity 7

1 1a blue/green **b** rice field **c** middle **d** one
Sample translation: The coolness, In the middle of a green rice field, one pine tree.

2 1a old **b** water **c** sound
Sample translation: An old pond, A frog dives in, The sound of water.

3 1a wind **b** water **c** blue
Sample translation: The evening breeze ..., water laps against the legs of a blue heron.

4 1a travel **b** man **c** needle
Sample translation: An autumn night ..., A travelling man's, Needlework.

Test yourself

Unit 1: tree, forest, wood, river, mountain, gold/money, fire, bamboo, rice field, stone

Unit 2: mouth, eye, woman, child, man, person, car, horse, like, gate

Unit 3: moon/month, sun/day, seven, ten, hundred, yen, thousand, ten thousand, year, nine

Unit 4: look/see/watch, listen, read, say, talk/speak, language, eat, drink, thing, go out/exit

Unit 6: row 1: old, small, big, high/tall/expensive, new, black, white, wide, cheap, blue
row 2: middle, above, below, country, meat, school, mother, father, rain, island

Unit 7: time, cultivated field, body, believe/trust, stay at, needle, turn/change, wicked/noisy, town, village

Unit 8: row 1: city/market, hall/large building, public, sake/alcohol, shop, fish, tea, garden, reside, station;
row 2: go/hold, inside, outside/foreign, seat, north, south, west, east, right, left
row 3: open, close

Index (1) Japanese–English: kanji charts

A unit-by-unit summary of main 漢字 including: number of strokes (in brackets), *on* and *kun* readings, English meanings and *jukugo* (compound word) examples.

- For stroke order of main 漢字, refer to the writing sections of each unit. The stroke order for those 漢字 in Units 1 and 2 which don't appear in the writing sections is given in these charts (labelled 'pic').
- *On* readings (*onyomi*) are given in capitals, *kun* readings (*kunyomi*) in lower case. The bracketed part of a *kun* reading indicates the part written in hiragana (dictionary form is given for verbs).

Unit 1

山	SAN, **yama;**	
(3)	*mountain*	
川	SEN, **kawa, gawa;**	
(3)	*river*	
日	NICHI, JITSU, **hi, bi, ka;**	
(4)	*day, sun*	
月	GETSU, GATSU, **tsuki;**	
(4)	*month, moon*	[pic.1]
土	DO, TO, **tsuchi;**	
(3)	*earth, ground*	
竹	CHIKU, **take;**	
(6)	*bamboo*	[pic.2]
木	MOKU, BOKU, **ki;**	
(4)	*tree, wood*	
林	RIN, **hayashi, bayashi;**	

(8)	*woods*	
森	SHIN, mori;	
(12)	*forest*	
水	SUI, mizu;	
(4)	*water*	
田	DEN, ta/da;	
(5)	*rice field*	
金	KIN, KON, kane;	
(8)	*gold, money*	[pic.3]
火	KA, hi, bi;	
(4)	*fire*	[pic.4]
石	SEKI, SHAKU, ishi, koku;	
(5)	*stone*	

pic.1

pic.2

pic.3

pic.4

Unit 2

口	KŌ, KU, kuchi, guchi;	
(3)	*mouth*	
足	SOKU (ZOKU), ashi, ta(riru);	
(7)	*foot (leg)*	[pic.5]
目	MOKU, me;	
(5)	*eye*	
女	JO, NYO, onna;	

	woman	[pic.6]
子 (3)	SHI, SU, ko; *child*	[pic.7]
人 (2)	NIN, JIN, hito; *person*	
耳 (6)	JI, mimi; *ear*	[pic.8]
手 (4)	SHU, te; *hand*	
力 (2)	RYOKU, RIKI, chikara; *power, strength*	[pic.9]
車 (7)	SHA, kuruma; *vehicle, car*	[pic.10]
馬 (10)	BA, uma; *horse*	[pic.11]
門 (8)	MON, kado; *gate*	
男 (7)	DAN, NAN, otoko; *man*	[pic.12]
好 (6)	KŌ, kono(mu); *like, love*	[pic.13]
明 (8)	MEI, MYŌ, aka(rui), aki(raka); *bright, light*	[pic.14]
本 (5)	HON, moto; *root, origin, main, book*	[pic.15]

pic.5

pic.6

pic.7

pic.8

pic.9

pic.10

pic.11

pic.12

pic.13

pic.14

pic.15

Unit 3

一
(1)
   ICHI, hito(tsu);
   one

二
(2)
   NI, futa(tsu);
   two

三
(3)
   SAN, mit(tsu);
   three

四
   SHI, yon, yo, yot(tsu);

(5)	*four*
五	GO, itsu(tsu);
(4)	*five*
六	ROKU, mut(tsu);
(4)	*six*
七	SHICHI, nana(tsu);
(2)	*seven*
八	HACHI, yat(tsu);
(2)	*eight*
九	KYŪ, KU; kokono(tsu);
(2)	*nine*
十	JŪ, tō;
(2)	*ten*
百	HYAKU;
(6)	*hundred*
千	SEN, chi;
(3)	*thousand*
万	MAN, BAN;
(3)	*ten thousand, all*
円	EN;
(4)	*yen, circle*
年	NEN, toshi;
(6)	*year, age*

Unit 4

聞	BUN, ki(ku);
(14)	*hear, listen*
見	KEN, mi(ru);
(7)	*look, see, watch*
書	SHO, ka(ku);
(10)	*write*
言	GEN, (GON), i(u), koto;
(7)	*say*
学	GAKU, mana(bu);
(8)	*study, learn*
買	BAI, ka(u);

(12)	*buy*
休	KYŪ, yasu(mu);
(6)	*rest*
出	SHUTSU, de(ru), da(su);
(5)	*go / come out*
売	BAI, u(ru);
(7)	*sell*
読	DOKU, yo(mu);
(14)	*read*
話	WA, hanashi, hana(su);
(13)	*talk*
食	SHOKU, ta(beru);
(9)	*eat*
飲	IN, no(mu);
(12)	*drink*
入	NYŪ, i(ru), hai(ru);
(2)	*enter, put in*
物	BUTSU, MOTSU, mono;
(8)	*thing*

Unit 6

立	RITSU, ta(tsu), tachi;
(5)	*stand (up)*
高	KŌ, taka(i);
(10)	*high, expensive*
鳥	CHŌ, tori;
(11)	*bird*
米	BEI, MAI, kome;
(6)	*rice*
大	DAI, TAI, ō(kii);
(3)	*big, great*
斤	KIN, ono;
(4)	*axe*
牛	GYŪ, ushi;
(4)	*cow, cattle*
古	KO, furu(i);

(5)
old

糸
SHI, ito;
(6)
thread

小
SHŌ, chii(sai), ko, o;
(3)
small

母
BO, haha, (o)kā(san);
(5)
mother

安
AN, yasu(i);
(6)
cheap, safe

広
KŌ, hiro(i);
(5)
wide, spacious

新
SHIN, atara(shii);
(13)
new

黒
KOKU, kuro(i);
(11)
black

白
HAKU, BYAKU, shiro(i), jiro;
(5)
white

青
SEI, SHŌ, ao(i);
(8)
blue, green, inexperienced

父
FU, chichi, tō, (o)tō(san);
(4)
father

雨
U, ame;
(8)
rain

上
JŌ, ue, nobo (ru), a(garu);
(3)
above, on, top

下
KA, GE, shita, moto, kuda(ru);
(3)
below, under, go down

中
CHŪ, naka;
(4)
inside, middle, within

雲
UN, kumo;
(12)
cloud

曇
DON, kumo(ri);
(16)
cloudy weather

雷
RAI, kaminari;
(13)
thunder

雪
SETSU, yuki;
(11)
snow

電
DEN;
(13)
electric

犬
(4)
KEN, inu;
dog

島
(10)
TŌ, shima, jima;
island

音
(9)
ON, IN, oto, ne;
sound

辛
(7)
SHIN, kara(i);
hot, bitter, spicy;

霜
(17)
SŌ, shimo;
frost

少
(4)
SHŌ, suku(nai), suko(shi);
few, a little

太
(4)
TAI, TA, futo(i);
fat, deep (voice)

国
(8)
KOKU, kuni, guni;
country

肉
(6)
NIKU;
meat, flesh

校
(10)
KŌ;
school

Unit 7

信
(9)
SHIN, shin(jiru);
believe, trust;

唱
(11)
SHŌ, tona(eru);
chant, recite;

畑
(9)
hata, hatake;
cultivated field

談
(15)
DAN;
talk, discussion

孫
(10)
SON, mago;
grandchild

鳴
(14)
MEI, na(ku);
cry, chirp

炎
(8)
EN, honō;
blaze, flame

焚 (12)	FUN, ta(ku), ya(ku); *burn, kindle*
語 (14)	GO; kata(ru); *language, word, tell*
埋 (10)	MAI, u(meru); *bury / be buried*
旦 (5)	TAN; *dawn*
姦 (9)	KAN; *wicked, noisy*
活 (9)	KATSU; *live, energy*
体 (7)	TAI, TEI, karada; *body*
町 (7)	CHŌ, machi; *town*
村 (7)	SON, mura; *village*
妹 (8)	MAI, imōto; *younger sister*
灯 (6)	TŌ, hi; *lamp, light*
折 (7)	SETSU, o(ru); *fold, snap, bend*
眠 (10)	MIN, nemu(i); *sleep(y)*
吠 (7)	HAI, ho(eru); *bark*
肘 (7)	CHŌ, hiji *elbow*
泊 (8)	HAKU, to(maru); *stay at, put up*
針 (10)	SHIN, hari; *needle*
転 (11)	TEN, koro(garu); *turn, change*
時 (10)	JI, toki, doki; *time*

Unit 8

店	TEN, **mise**;
(8)	*shop, store*
屋	OKU, **ya**;
(9)	*shop*
局	KYOKU;
(7)	*bureau, office*
所	SHO, JO, **tokoro**;
(8)	*place*
場	JŌ, **ba**;
(12)	*place*
館	KAN;
(16)	*hall, large building*
園	EN, **sono**;
(13)	*garden*
市	SHI, **ichi**;
(5)	*city, market*
工	KŌ, KU;
(3)	*construction*
公	KŌ, **ōyake**;
(4)	*public*
図	TO, ZU, **haka(ru)**;
(7)	*drawing, map*
魚	GYO, **sakana, uo**;
(11)	*fish*
酒	SHU, **sake, saka**;
(10)	*rice wine, alcohol*
茶	CHA;
(9)	*tea*
薬	YAKU, **kusuri**;
(16)	*medicine*
洗	SEN, **ara(u)**;
(9)	*wash*
主	SHU, **nushi**;
(5)	*master, owner*
駐	CHŪ;
(15)	*reside, stop-over*

住 (7)	JŪ, su(mu); *reside, live*
駅 (14)	EKI; *station*
便 (9)	BEN, BIN; *convenience, mail*
行 (6)	KŌ, GYŌ, AN, i(ku), yu(ku), okona(u); *go, hold*
室 (9)	SHITSU; *room*
内 (4)	NAI, DAI, uchi; *inside, home*
外 (5)	GAI, GE, soto, hoka; *outside, foreign*
席 (10)	SEKI; *seat, place*
料 (10)	RYŌ; *charge, materials*
北 (5)	HOKU, BOKU, kita; *north*
南 (9)	NAN, minami; *south*
東 (8)	TŌ, higashi; *east*
西 (6)	SEI, SAI, nishi; *west*
禁 (13)	KIN; *forbidden*
右 (5)	U, YŪ, migi; *right*
左 (5)	SA, hidari; *left*
開 (12)	KAI, a(keru), hira(ku); *open*
閉 (11)	HEI, shi(meru), to(jiru); *close*

Index (2) English–Japanese: word index

The number in brackets indicates the section where the word first appears.

A

above (6.4)   abroad (8.7)   absence from school (4.5)   academic ability (4.5)   address (8.6)   admission free (8.7)   adult (6.6) alcohol (8.4)   a little (6.5)   America (6.7)   arrival (8.11)   art (8.4)   art gallery (8.4)   ask (7.6)   axe (6.2)

B

bad at (6.6)   bamboo (1.2)   bamboo shoots (4.4)   bank (8.6) bar (8.4)   bark (7.4)   bathroom (8.8)   beckon (7.6)   beef (6.7)   believe (7.3)   below (6.4)   bicycle (8.7)   big (6.2) bird (6.2)   bitter (6.5)   black (6.3)   blaze (7.3)   blue (6.3)   blue-white (6.6)   body (7.4)   book (4.5)   bookshop (8.4)   boy (2.4, 6.6)   branch (7.7)   break (7.4)   bright (2.4, 7.6)   brush (4.3)   bullet train (8.12)   bureau (8.4)   burn (7.3)   bury (7.3) be buried (7.3)   buy (4.2)   buyer (4.5)   buying and selling (4.5)

C

calf (6.6)   car (2.3)   car park (8.6)   carriage (2.4)   cart (2.3) Central America (6.7)   certificate (7.4)   chant (7.3)   cheap (6.3)   chicken (6.7)   child (2.3, 6.6)   China (6.7)   chirp (7.3) cinema (8.6)   city (8.4)   cleanse (7.6)   clear (7.6)   clear up (7.6) close (8.11)   closed (8.11)   cloud (6.5)   cloudy weather (6.5) clue (6.6)   coffee shop (8.4)   construction (8.4) convenience (8.6)   conversation (7.4)   cosmetics (8.8) country (6.7)   cow (6.2)   create (7.6)   cry (animal) (7.3) cultivated field (7.3)

D

dawn (7.3)   day (1.1)   dealer (4.5)   decree (7.6)   departure (8.11)   discussion (7.3)   dog (6.5)   domestic (8.7)   dormant volcano (4.5)   dove (6.5)   down (8.3)   drawing (8.4)   drink (4.3)   drinking place (8.4)   drinking water (4.5)   drinks (4.5)   drought (7.6)   dry weather (7.6)   dwell (8.6)

E

ear (2.3)   earth (1.2)   east (8.9)   eat (4.3)   eating and drinking (4.5)   eight (3.2)   elbow (7.4)   electric (6.5)   elementary school (6.7)   emotion (7.6)   enter (4.3)   entrance (4.5)   entrance fee (8.7)   exit (4.5)   explosion (7.6)   express (8.12)   eye (2.3)

F

factory (8.4)   fare adjustment office (8.6)   fat (6.5)   father (6.3) fee (8.7)   feeling (7.6)   few (6.5)   fine weather (7.6)   fire (1.3) fish (8.4)   fishmonger (8.4)   five (3.2)   flame (7.3)   flesh (6.7) fold (7.4)   food (4.3, 4.5)   foot (2.3)   forbidden (8.10) foreign (8.7)   foreign exchange (8.7)   forest (1.3)   four (3.2) Friday (1.4)   frost (6.5)

G

garden (8.4)   gate (2.3)   gateway (2.4)   girl (2.4, 6.6)   go (8.6)   go in (4.3)   going in and out (4.5)   gold (1.3)   good at (6.6)   go out (4.2)   grandchild (7.3)   greengrocer (8.4)   grilled (8.12)   ground (1.3)

H

hall (8.4)   hand (2.3)   hear (4.2)   heavy rain (6.6)   high (6.2)   high school (6.7)   history (7.4)   hold (7.6)   holiday (4.2, 4.5)   horse (2.3)   horse power (2.4)   hot (6.5)   hour (7.4)   hundred (3.4)

I

imperial edict (7.6)   information (8.6)   inherit (7.6)   inn,
Japanese (8.6)   inside (6.4)   international phone (8.7)   invite
(7.6)   island (6.5)   island country (6.7)   items for sale (4.5)

J

Japan (2.4)   Japanese: bath (8.8), cuisine (8.8), inn (8.6), person
(2.4), room (8.7), style (8.8)   junior high school (6.7)

K

kindle (7.3)   kiosk (8.4)

L

lamp (7.4)   language (7.4)   large building (8.4)   left (8.11)   left
luggage (8.7)   lesson (7.4)   library (8.4)   like (15)   listen (4.2)
liquor store (8.4)   live (7.4)   liver (7.6)   long-distance train
(8.7)   look (4.2)   love (2.4)   luggage (8.7)

M

make (7.6)   mail (8.6)   man (2.4)   manpower (2.4)   map
(8.4)   market (8.4, 8.5)   marsh (7.6)   master (8.6)   meat (6.7)
medicine (8.4)   middle (6.4)   middle school (6.7)   mischief
(7.6)   Monday (1.4)   money (1.3)   money exchange (8.6)
month (1.1)   mother (6.3)   mother country (6.7)   mountain
(1.3)   moon (1.1)   mouth (2.3)   museum (8.6)

N

narrative (7.4)   needle (7.4)   new (6.3)   new car (6.6)
newspaper (6.6)   new year (6.6)   nine (3.2)   noise (6.5)   north
(8.9)   not allowed (8.10)

O

occupied taxi (8.7)   office (8.4)   old (6.2)   older (6.6)   one (3.2)
on top (6.4)   open (8.11)   open for business (8.11)   origin (2.4)

P

paddy field (2.4)   pair (4.5)   pale (6.6)   parcel (8.7)   parents
(6.6)   park (8.4)   passport control (8.7)   person (2.3)   perspire
(7.6)   pharmacy (8.4)   pigeon (6.5)   place (8.4)   poem (7.4)
pointed (6.5)   pole (7.6)   polished rice (6.6)   population (2.4)
post office (8.6)   powder room (8.8)   power (2.3)   previous
(7.6)   primary school (6.7)   proof (7.4)   public (8.4)   public
eye, in the (2.5)   pull (8.11)   puppy (6.6)   purify (7.6)   purity
(7.6)   push (8.11)

R

rain (6.3)   read (4.3)   reading (4.5)   recite (7.3)   request (7.6)
reserved seat (8.7)   reside (8.6)   rest (4.2)   restrain (7.6)
rice (6.2)   rice field (1.3)   rickshaw (2.4)   right (8.11)   river
(1.3)   rod (7.6)   roof (8.4)   room (8.7)   root (2.4)   rotate (7.4)

S

safe (6.3)   samurai (7.6)   Saturday (1.4)   say (4.2)   school
(6.7)   seat (8.7)   second-hand car (6.6)   sell (4.3)   seller (4.5)
set meal (8.7)   seven (3.2)   shop (8.4)   shopping (4.5)   shopping
area (8.6)   sightseeing (4.5)   six (3.2)   sleep (7.4)   sleeper
train (8.7)   small (6.2)   small dog (6.6)   smoke (8.10)   snap
(7.4)   snore (7.6)   snow (6.5)   soar (7.6)   sound (6.5)   south
(8.9)   spacious (6.3)   speak (4.3)   special express (8.12)   spirit
(7.6)   stand (news) (8.4)   stand (up) (6.2)   start school (4.5)
station (8.6)   stay at (7.4)   stone (1.3)   store (8.4)   strength
(2.3)   strictly forbidden (8.10)   study (4.2)   study visit (4.5)
Sunday (1.4)   superiors (6.6)   swamp (7.6)   swan (6.6)

T

talk (4.3)   tall (6.2)   tapered (6.5)   tea (8.4)   teashop (8.4)
telephone (6.6)   temple (7.4)   ten (3.2)   ten thousand (3.4)
theatre (8.6)   thing (4.5)   thousand (3.4)   thread (6.2)   three
(3.2)   thunder (6.5)   Thursday (1.4)   ticket office (8.6)   time
(7.4)   toilet (8.4, 8.5, 8.8)   tower (7.6)   town (7.4)   train (6.6)
translation (7.4)   travel (8.6)   tree (1.3)   Tuesday (1.4)   tune
(7.4)   turn (7.4)   two (3.2)

U

under (6.4)   underground (8.12)   university (6.6)   unoccupied
taxi (8.7)   unreserved seat (8.7)   up (8.3)

V

vast (6.6)   vehicle (2.3)   village (7.4)   vinegar (7.6)
volcano (2.4)

W

wait (8.8)   waiting room (8.8)   wash (8.4)   watch (4.2)   water
(1.2)   water power (2.4)   Wednesday (1.4)   west (8.9)   Western-
style (8.8), cuisine (8.8), room (8.7)   white (6.3)   white rice
(6.6, 7.6)   wickedness (7.3, 7.6)   wide (6.3)   wine (8.4)   wine
shop (8.4)   woman (2.3)   wood(s) (1.2)   words (4.2)   write
(4.3)   writing (4.5)

Y

yen (3.4)   year (3.5)   yesterday (7.6)   younger sister (7.4)
youth (6.6)

Taking it further

There is a wealth of workbooks, internet sites and software packages that can help you to take your study of Japanese script further. The suggestions below are taken from my own teaching experience and feedback from students and other teachers. It is by no means an exhaustive list, and the internet in particular is continuously producing new and often improved possibilities. However, the list does include some of the real 'backbones' and classics for learning to read and write Japanese.

Books

1 Spoken language

Try other titles in Hodder and Stoughton's **Teach yourself series**:

- *Get started in Japanese*, Helen Gilhooly, 2010. This includes a chapter on script.
- *Speak Japanese*, Helen Gilhooly, 2010
- *Fast-track Japanese*, Elisabeth Smith, 2010
- *Complete Japanese*, Helen Gilhooly, 2010. Includes unit-by-unit sections on reading script.

2 Written language – kana scripts

There are various good *kana* workbooks which take you systematically through the learning process, including the following:

- *Easy Hiragana*, Fujihiko Kaneda et al., McGraw-Hill, 1989
- *Easy Katakana*, Tina Wells et al., McGraw-Hill, 1989

- *Let's Learn Hiragana, Let's Learn Katakana* (2 volumes), YK Mitamura, Kodansha Europe, 1992
- *Hiragana Gambatte*, Katakana Gambatte (2 volumes), Deleece Batt, Kodansha Europe, 1994. Teaches through manga-style art and mini-articles on Japanese society and culture.
- *Hiragana/Katakana in 48 minutes* (2 volumes), Hiroko C. Quackenbush et al., Curriculum Corporation, 1989. Set of flashcards for memorizing kana through picture and sound association.
- *Introduction to Written Japanese* (2 volumes), Jim Gleeson, Tuttle Language Library, 1997
- *Kana Can Be Easy*, Kunihiko Ogawa, The Japan Times, 1992. Teaches kana through mnemonics and picture stories.
- *All About Katakana*, Anne M. Stewart, Kodansha Europe, 1993. How to memorize katakana quickly, with over 1,000 examples of its usage.

3 Written language – kanji

- *250 Essential Kanji for Everyday Use*, Tuttle & Co., 1998. Includes many illustrations and photos of everyday kanji, such as signs and maps, as well as stroke order, readings and compounds of 250 common kanji.
- *Basic Kanji Book 500* (2 volumes), Chieko Kano et al., Bonjinsha. A workbook which introduces 12–15 themed kanji per chapter with background stories and exercises to help consolidate learning.
- *Essential Kanji*, P.G. O'Neil, Weatherhill, 1974. A systematic reference book of the 2,000 essential kanji.
- *A Guide to Remembering the Japanese Characters*, Kenneth G. Henshall, Tuttle & Co., 1998. Another systematic reference, which also includes mnemonics and stories to explain the development of each kanji and help you to remember them.
- *Remembering the Kanji*, James W. Heisig, Japan Publications Trading Company, 1990. This course teaches you how to remember kanji through imaginative and memorable pictures and stories.

- *Let's Learn Kanji*, J.Y. and Y.K. Mitamura, 1997. A new approach to learning 250 basic kanji through radicals and components.
- *Japan in Your Pocket – Illustrated Japanese Characters*, Japan Travel Bureau, Inc. 1993. A pocket-sized book which introduces everyday kanji via their radicals in an easy-to-read format.
- *Read Japanese Today*, Len Walsh, Tuttle & Co., 1969. Another pocket-sized book which introduces kanji through pictures and mnemonics.

4 Texts and readers (for intermediate and advanced learners)

- *Kanji from the Start, a Comprehensive Japanese Reader*, Martin Lam and Shimizu Kaoru, Kodansha International, 1995. This introduces new kanji in each chapter, along with text incorporating them plus grammar explanations.
- *An Introduction to Newspaper Japanese*, O. and N. Mizutami, Japan Times, 1986. Helps the intermediate learner decipher newspaper headings and articles.
- *Tottochan*, Kuroyanagi Tetsuko, Kodansha. The best-selling novel of the author's school life in 1950s Japan which is available in Japanese, English and bilingual versions.
- *Dondon Yomeru, Iroirona Hanashi*, Akimoto Miharu, 1991. This is a compilation of simplified short stories by famous Japanese novelists.

The Kodansha *Power Japanese* series has a number of Japanese readers including:

- *Kanji Idioms*, George Wallace and Kayoko Kimiya, 1995 – introduces lots of four-character compound words with explanations and translations of their use.
- *Read Real Japanese*, Janet Ashby, 1994 – a series of short essays with English translations and grammar explanations from

famous Japanese personalities such as the musician, Sakamoto Ryuichi and the female novelist, Yoshimoto Banana.

5 *Magazines (available from Japanese bookshops)*

- *Hiragana Times* (monthly). Written in kana, kanji and English and aimed at cross-cultural communication. Has its own website: www.hiraganatimes.com.
- *Mangajin* (quarterly). Extracts from popular Japanese comics with translation, grammar and cultural explanations in English.

6 *Dictionaries*

- *The Oxford Starter Japanese Dictionary*, Jonathan Bunt, Oxford University Press, 2000. Two-way dictionary especially written for students of Japanese, with examples of how the words are used in practice. Entries in script and English.
- *Webster's New World Compact Japanese Dictionary*, 1997. Two-way dictionary, entries in rōmaji, script and English.
- *Pictorial Japanese and English Dictionary*, ed. John Pheby, Oxford University Press, 1997
- *Dictionary of Basic Japanese Grammar*, S. Makino and M. Tsutsui, The Japan Times, 1992
- *Kodansha Kanji Learner's Dictionary*, Jack Halpern, Kodansha International, 2002
- *The New Nelson Japanese–English Character Dictionary*, Andrew N. Nelson, Tuttle & Co, 1997. An update of the classic kanji dictionary with contemporary definitions.
- *The Compact Nelson, Japanese–English Character Dictionary*, John H. Haig, Tuttle & Co. A portable version of Nelson's classic kanji dictionary.
- *The Kanji Dictionary*, Mark Spahn and Wolfgang Hadamitzky, Tuttle & Co, 1996. 47,000+ kanji compounds.
- *Canon Wordtank Super Electronic Dictionary*. Electronic dictionaries are very popular in Japan, but are created mainly for Japanese native speakers. The *Canon Wordtank* is for

foreign learners of Japanese, and features include two-way
dictionaries, kanji dictionary and useful expressions.

7 General

- *World Cultures: Japan*, Helen Gilhooly, Hodder and Stoughton,
  2002. For a general introduction to all aspects of Japanese life
  and society.
- *Kodansha Bilingual Encyclopedia of Japan*, 1998. An easy-
  to-read comprehensive encyclopedia with entries and index in
  English and Japanese.
- *Kodansha Encyclopedia of Japan*, 1999. A detailed and
  comprehensive English-language reference book on all aspects of
  Japan. Also available on CD-ROM with various extras such as
  dictionary and links to worldwide web.
- *Japan Made Easy – All You Need to Know to Enjoy Japan*, Boye
  Lafayette De Mente, Passport Books, 1995. Practical advice and
  information for visiting Japan including lots of do's and don'ts.
- *Japan*, Chris Taylor, Lonely Planet, 1997. Traveller's guidebook
  includes lots of interesting facts and advice about Japan.

Websites

The internet is constantly changing and developing, and it is always
worth doing searches for new Japanese language sites; some good
current ones include:

- *Jim Breen's Japanese Page*: www.csse.monash.edu.au/~jwb/
  japanese.html or www.csse.monash.edu.au/~jwb/cgi-bin/
  wwwjdic.cgi?1C to go direct to dictionary (or do a search for
  Jim Breen). This site includes instructions on how to download
  a freeware Japanese word-processing programme (JWPce),
  a Japanese–English dictionary and links to many other Japanese
  learning sites and free-/shareware.

- For information on the Japanese Language Proficiency Tests (there are four levels from beginners to advanced): www.soas.ac.uk/languagecentre/awards/jlpt/
- For information about the three scripts: www.learn-japanese-kanji-hiragana-katakana.com/katakana.htm

---

Software

- All Apple Macs have the capability for you to type in Japanese script (refer to the user manual for details); Microsoft PCs post-2000 have the capability for you to type in Japanese characters using global IME, and you can download global IME with older PCs. You need to open up language settings in order to activate global IME, but if you have any problems, visit: www.microsoft.com/windows/ie/ie6/downloads/ recommended/ime/install.mspx to find out how to download global IME.

There is also software for learning or inputting Japanese script. Of course, the technology changes all the time, but there follows a list of some of the best learning software produced for Japanese at time of print:

- *Kanakun*, Fujitsu, Aus 1998, CD-ROM. *Hiragana* and *Katakana* tutor which has animated stroke order, pronunciation practice and lots of recognition games.
- *Kantaro*, Macquarie University, Sydney, Fujitsu 1993, CD-ROM × 3. Interactive kanji-learning program which teaches kanji through picture association and includes writing practice, readings and compounds.
- *Kanji Sensei* 3.0, Frank Potter, 1996, Pacific Rim Systems, 2 × floppy disks. This is becoming more difficult to get hold of, and it is only available on floppy disks, which not many computers can access these days. However, if yours can, it is worth persisting because it is an excellent kanji tutor

which works systematically and thematically through basic kanji, giving stroke-order demonstrations and practice and opportunities to test yourself against the computer tutor.

- *Free Light Japanese*, Chilly Mazarin, Free Light software, 1995, CD-ROM. A Japanese-learning program for Windows which teaches *hiragana*, *katakana* and *kanji* with drills and pictures.
- *Blackbelt Japanese*, Rising Wave Inc., Honolulu 1995, CD-ROM. Language-learning games for recognition (but not writing practice) of the Japanese writing system.
- *Talk Now! Learn Japanese*, Eurotalk Interactive, London 1998, CD-ROM. Beginners' conversational Japanese but adapted from European languages, so not culturally specific.

There are also a number of Japanese word-processing packages available which either work independently of Windows or are Windows compatible. They can also be used for sending e-mail in Japanese (providing the receiver has compatible software). The ones below also have other features such as dictionaries and *kanji* look-up facilities:

- *NJStar*, NJStar Software Corp., 1991–99. Information (including downloadable trial program) available at their website at www.njstar.com. This package works separately to Windows, but it is possible to cut and paste into Windows and it has a range of advanced features, such as various fonts and dictionaries.
- *Kanji Kit 2000*, Japanese Utility for English Windows, Pacific Software Publishing, Inc.: www.kanjikit.net. Works with many Windows applications, such as Photoshop, Corel Draw, Internet Explorer, MS Excel/Word, etc. Can be used to create Japanese sites and customized *kanji* characters.
- *JWPce* (see website section above for contact details). A basic word-processing package for typing in Japanese script (works separately to Windows), but with useful features such as dictionaries and *kanji* search facility.

Organizations

- Japanese embassies across the world have JICC (Japan Information and Cultural Centres) from which you can borrow books and videos as well as subscribe to a number of magazines and newsletters and find out about Japanese classes, societies and other organizations in your country. Go to www.mofa.go.jp/about/emb_cons/mofaserv.html and you will find links to every JICC and Japanese embassy in the world.
- Japan National Tourist Organization (JNTO): www.jnto.go.jp
- For information on the JET programme (teaching English in Japan): www.jetprogramme.org